THE CATHEDRAL OF SAINT PAUL

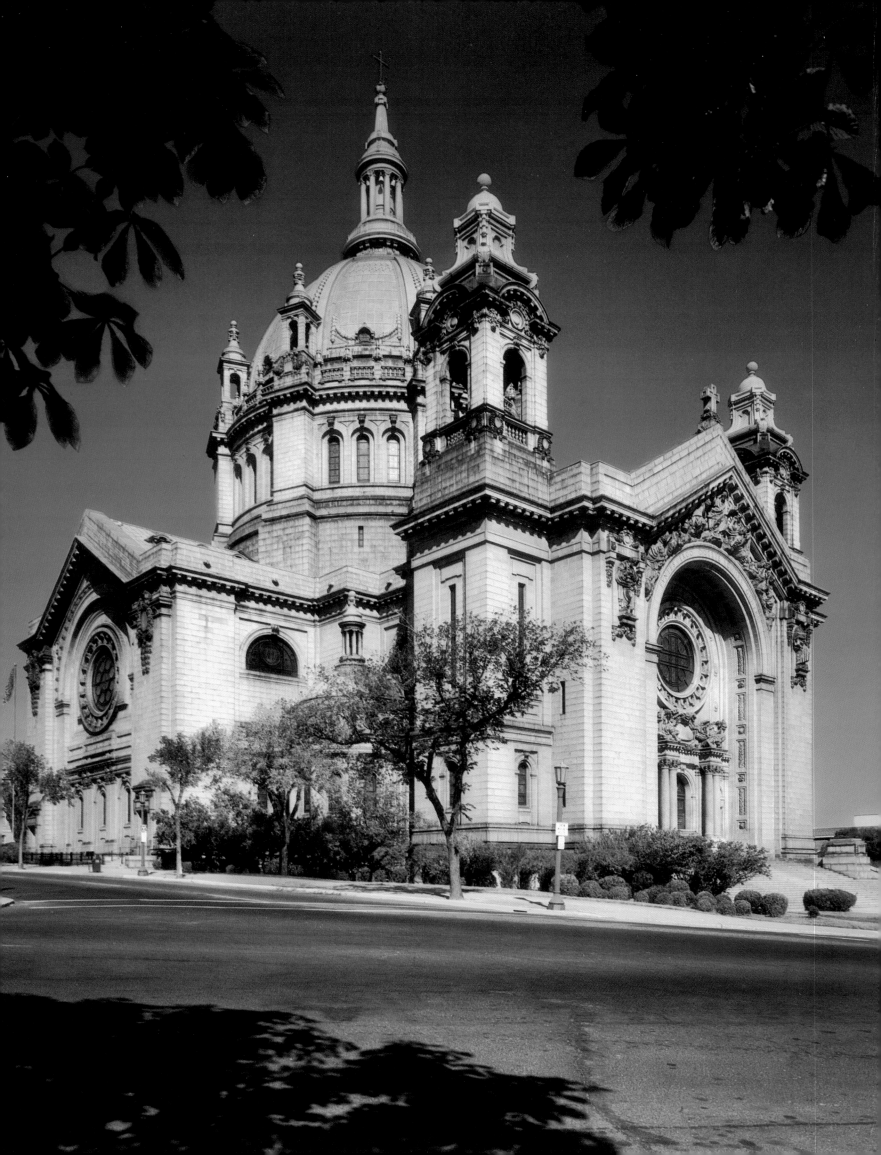

THE CATHEDRAL OF SAINT PAUL
AN ARCHITECTURAL BIOGRAPHY

Eric C. Hansen

The Cathedral of Saint Paul
St. Paul, Minnesota 1990

CREDITS

Illustrations were supplied by the following agencies and individuals: Archives of the Cathedral of Saint Paul, Frontispiece, 1.1., 1.2, 2.5, 2.6, 3.2, 3.3, 3.4, 3.5, 3.6, 4.3, 4.4, 4.5, 4.6, 4.7, 4.8, 4.9, 4.10, 4.11, 4.12, 4.13, p. 41, 5.1, 5.2, 5.6, 6.1, 6.2, 6.4, 6.7, 6.8, 6.11, 6.15, 6.16, 6.17, 6.18, 6.27, 6.29, 8.1, 8.8, 8.9, p. 137; *Catholic Bulletin,* 6.34, 8.6; Reverend Paul LaFontaine, 6.6, 7.17, 7.18, 7.19, 7.20; Minnesota Historical Society, 2.1, 2.2, 2.3, 2.4, 3.1, 4.2; Joseph Oden, 5.5, pp. 49, 120; Office of Communications, Archdiocese of St. Paul and Minneapolis, 8.10, 8.11; John Perrone, 5.3, 5.4, 6.3, 6.19, 6.20, 6.21, 6.22, 6.23, 6.24, 6.28, 7.2, 7.7, 7.8, 7.9, 7.12, 7.16, 7.21, 7.26, 7.27, 7.28, 7.34, 7.35, 8.5; Philip Prowse, pp. 1, 3, 9, 2.7, p. 17, 3.7, 3.8, p. 29, 6.5, 6.9, 6.10, 6.12, 6.13, 6.14, 6.25, 6.26, 6.30, 6.31, 6.32, 6.33, p. 79, 7.1, 7.3, 7.4, 7.5, 7.6, 7.10, 7.11, 7.13, 7.14, 7.15, 7.22, 7.23, 7.24, 7.25, 7.29, 7.30, 7.31, 7.32, 7.33, 7.36, p. 103, 8.2, 8.3, 8.4, pp. 115, 127; *St. Paul Pioneer Press Dispatch,* 4.1, 8.12.

Publication of this book has been aided by generous financial grants from the following: the Patrick and Aimee Butler Family Foundation; First Bank System Foundation; McGough Construction Company, Inc.; Gerald Rauenhorst Family Foundation; Carl A. Weyerhauser 1986 Charitable Term Trust; and the College of St. Thomas.

ISBN 0-9625765-0-6
Library of Congress Catalog Card Number: 90-80194
Printed in the United States of America
Design: Bill Lundborg

To

Rt. Rev. Msgr. Lawrence F. Ryan
Rector of the Cathedral of Saint Paul, 1916-1940

In Memoriam

and

Rev. Msgr. Terrence J. Murphy
President of the College of St. Thomas

John G. Nemo, Ph.D.
Dean of the College of St. Thomas

and

William M. Delehanty, Ph.D.
Associate Professor of History
College of St. Thomas

Ad Multos Annos

CONTENTS

Illustrations. ix

Foreword xi

Acknowledgements xiii

Introduction. 1

Chapter One 3

Chapter Two 9

Chapter Three 17

Chapter Four 29

Chapter Five. 41

Chapter Six 49

Chapter Seven 79

Chapter Eight 103

Conclusion 115

Notes 123

Appendices 127

Bibliography 133

Index 134

ILLUSTRATIONS

The Cathedral of Saint Paul   Frontispiece

INTRODUCTION

The Cathedra *of the Cathedral of Saint Paul*   1

CHAPTER ONE

The Crozier of Archbishop John Ireland   3
1.1 *Archbishop John Ireland*   6
1.2 *Emmanuel Louis Masqueray*   7

CHAPTER TWO

Our Lady of Victory   9
2.1 *Father Lucien Galtier*   11
2.2 *Father Augustine Ravoux*   12
2.3 *The Log Chapel of Saint Paul, with addition, 1847* 13
2.4 *Bishop Joseph Cretin*   14
2.5 *The Second Cathedral of Saint Paul*   14
2.6 *The Third Cathedral of Saint Paul*   16
2.7 *Bishop Thomas Langdon Grace*   16

CHAPTER THREE

*The Metropolitan Processional Cross of Archbishop
    John Ireland*   17
3.1 *The Kittson Mansion, c. 1895*   20
3.2 *The Executive Building Committee*   21
3.3 *The Ground Plan (Masqueray)*   24
3.4 *The Front Elevation (Masqueray)*   25
3.5 *The Interior (Masqueray)*   26
3.6 *The Side Elevation (Masqueray)*   26
3.7 *The Cathedral of Saint Paul. The Exterior*   27
3.8 *The Cathedral of Saint Paul. The Interior*   27

CHAPTER FOUR

*A Souvenir of the Laying of the Cornerstone,
    June 2, 1907*   29
4.1 *Plan for the Rerouting of Summit Avenue at the
    Site of the New Cathedral, 1906*   31
4.2 *Entrance to the Selby Avenue Tunnel*   32
4.3 *Setting the Foundation, 1906*   33
4.4 *Work on the Upper Foundation, 1907*   34
4.5 *The Laying of the Cornerstone, June 2, 1907*   35
4.6 *Father (later Bishop) John J. Lawler*   36
4.7 *Erection of the Granite Cross on the Facade,
    July 18, 1912*   37
4.8 *The Superstructure under Construction*   38
4.9 *The Dome under Construction, 1912*   38
4.10 *The Framing of the Lantern on the Dome, 1912*   38
4.11 *The Facade with Uncarved Tympanum, 1912*   39
4.12 Christ and the Apostles Flanked by Saints Peter
    and Paul. *Detail from the Sculpture of the
    Facade*   40
4.13 Faith and Science. *Detail from the Sculpture of the
    Facade*   40

CHAPTER FIVE

The Chapel of St. Peter. St. Peter   41
5.1 *The Final Mass in the Third Cathedral of Saint
    Paul, August 30, 1914*   43
5.2 *The Chapel of St. Peter, 1916-1917*   45
5.3 *The Chapel of St. Peter. Detail of the Ceiling*   46
5.4 *The Chapel of St. Joseph, 1916-1918*   47
5.5 *Masqueray's Grave Marker, Calvary Cemetery,
    St. Paul*   48
5.6 *The Funeral of Archbishop Ireland,
    October 2, 1918*   48

CHAPTER SIX

St. Paul. *Detail from the Baldachin*   49
6.1 *Archbishop Austin Dowling*   51
6.2 *Monsignor Lawrence F. Ryan*   51
6.3 *The Chapel of the Blessed Virgin Mary, 1914-1919* 53
6.4 *The Main Altar with Its Pre-1940 Setting*   54
6.5 *The Baldachin*   54
6.6 *The Sanctuary Seen from the Base of the Dome*   56
6.7 *The Sacristy, 1924*   57
6.8 *The Sacristy. Detail of the Exterior Decoration*   57
6.9 *The Sacristy. Angel in Prayer*   58
6.10 *The Sacristy. Detail of the Cabinets*   58
6.11 *The Sacristy. Interior of the Dome*   59
6.12 *The Sanctuary Apse. The Seven Gifts of the Holy
    Spirit*   59
6.13 *The Bronze Shield in the Sanctuary Containing the
    Archdiocesan Coat of Arms*   60
6.14 *The Choir Stalls*   60
6.15 *The Pulpit*   61
6.16 *The Te Deum Grilles. Panels I-III (South Side of
    the Ambulatory)*   62
6.17 *The Te Deum Grilles. Panel V (North Side of the
    Ambulatory).*   62
6.18 *The Te Deum Grilles. Detail of Panel II (North
    Side of the Ambulatory)*   63
6.19 *The Shrine of St. Patrick, 1926-1928*   64
6.20 *The Shrine of St. Boniface, 1926-1928*   65
6.21 *The Shrine of St. Anthony, 1926-1928*   66
6.22 *The Shrine of St. John the Baptist, 1926-1928*   67
6.23 *The Shrine of Sts. Cyril and Methodius, 1926-1928* 68
6.24 *The Shrine of St. Therese of Lisieux, 1926-1928*   69
6.25 *The Ambulatory*   70
6.26 *The Organ Screen over the Sacristy Entrance*   71
6.27 *Archbishop John Gregory Murray*   72
6.28 *The Chapel of the Sacred Heart, 1931-1933*   73
6.29 *The Unfinished Interior as seen during the
    Installation of Austin Dowling as Second
    Archbishop of St. Paul, March 25, 1919*   74
6.30 *The Narthex looking North*   75
6.31 *The Baptistry*   76

6.32 *Title Page of the Memorial Volume in the Founders'*
    Chapel   77
6.33 *A Typical Page from the Memorial Volume in the*
    Founders' Chapel   77
6.34 *Cardinal Pacelli at the Cathedral of Saint Paul,*
    October 27, 1936   78

CHAPTER SEVEN

    The Lamb of God. *Detail from the East Rose*
        Window   79
7.1 *The Chapel of St. Peter.* St. Peter *and* Benedict XV   81
7.2 *The Chapel of the Blessed Virgin Mary.* The
    Crucifixion   82
7.3 *The Shrines of the Nations.* St. Clare   82
7.4 *The Shrines of the Nations.* St. Columbin   83
7.5 *The Shrines of the Nations.* St. Bridget   83
7.6 *The Shrines of the Nations.* St. Wenceslaus   83
7.7 *The Sanctuary.* The Eucharist   85
7.8 *The Sanctuary.* Penance   85
7.9 The Resurrection *(The East Rose Window)*   86
7.10 St. James. *Detail from the East Rose Window*   87
7.11 St. John. *Detail from the East Rose Window*   87
7.12 The Beatitudes *(The South Rose Window)*   88
7.13 Blessed Catherine Tekakwitha. *Detail from the*
    South Rose Window   89
7.14 St. Frances Xavier Cabrini. *Detail from the South*
    Rose Window   89
7.15 St. Peter Claver. *Detail from the South Rose*
    Window   89
7.16 The American Jesuit Martyrs *(The North Rose*
    Window)   90
7.17 Mary, Queen of Martyrs. *Detail from the North*
    Rose Window   91
7.18 The Death of St. John de Brébeuf. *Detail from the*
    North Rose Window   91
7.19 The Death of St. Gabriel Lalemant. *Detail from*
    the North Rose Window   91
7.20 A Bear. *Detail from the North Rose Window*   91
7.21 *The Chapel of St. Joseph.* The Presentation   91
7.22 St. John Vianney, the Christ of Revelation, St.
    Mary Magdalene *(South Confessional Windows)*   92
7.23 St. John Nepomucene, Christ the Good Shepherd,
    St. Dismas *(North Confessional Windows)*   93
7.24 *The Founders' Chapel.* History of the
    Administration of the Sacraments in the
    Archdiocese of St. Paul: Matrimony and the
    Eucharist   94
7.25 St. Anthony Mary Claret *and* St. Pius X *(Lower*
    East Transept Windows)   95

7.26 *The Dome.* Angels   96
7.27 *The Sacristy.* Christ the High Priest   96
7.28 *The Sacristy.* The Immaculate Conception   96
7.29 *Théodule-Augustin Ribot,* The Entombment,
    undated   97
7.30 *Nicholas Richard Brewer,* Crucifixion, *undated*   98
7.31 *Karl-Ernest-Rodolphe-Heinrich-Salem Lehmann,*
    The Descent from the Cross, *1867*   99
7.32 St. Mark *(Southeastern Pier)*   100
7.33 St. Matthew *(Southwestern Pier)*   100
7.34 St. John *(Northwestern Pier)*   100
7.35 St. Luke *(Northeastern Pier)*   101
7.36 *The Present System of Interior Lighting*   102

CHAPTER EIGHT

    The Commemoration of the Cathedral's Consecra-
        tion, October 14, 1958, carved into the Tinos
        marble of the Southeastern (lower Selby Avenue)
        Vestibule   103
8.1 *Monsignor George E. Ryan*   105
8.2 *The Gilded Interior of the Dome*   106
8.3 *Pendentive of the Dome.* Justice   107
8.4 *Pendentive of the Dome.* Temperance   108
8.5 *One of the Fourteen Stations of the Cross*   108
8.6 *Monsignor George E. Ryan with one of the twelve*
    crosses commemorating the consecration of
    October 14, 1958   109
8.7 *President John F. Kennedy arrives for eleven o'clock*
    Mass at the Cathedral, October 7, 1962   109
8.8 *The Exterior Lighting System*   110
8.9 *The Interior under Restoration, 1976-1977*   112
8.10 *The Five New Bells Stand in the Cathedral Parking*
    Lot Awaiting Installation   113
8.11 *John R. Roach, Seventh Archbishop of St. Paul and*
    Minneapolis, after the Blessing of the Bells, June
    7, 1987   113
8.12 *The Installation of the Bell Dedicated to the Blessed*
    Virgin Mary   114

CONCLUSION

    The Paschal Candlestick   115
    Church and State in the City of St. Paul   118

NOTES/APPENDICES/BIBLIOGRAPHY

    Christmas at the Cathedral of Saint Paul   120
    The West Wall of the Founders' Chapel   127

    The Cathedral of Saint Paul: The Selby Avenue Side   137

FOREWORD

The publication of *The Cathedral of Saint Paul: An Architectural Biography* comes in response to an ever growing number of requests from the many people who are struck by its beauty. In addition to those who join our Cathedral parishioners for worship, a steady stream of thousands of visitors and tourists come by car and bus to see this work of truly remarkable architecture. Its story is one of a strong and vibrant faith that led Archbishop Ireland and his people to build "a Great Church for a Great City."

You will enjoy this scholarly yet readable book and you will delight in the many illustrations which reveal the Cathedral's beauty.

I am very grateful to Dr. Eric C. Hansen, who has written a book which will be a lasting credit to this building. As we approach the seventy-fifth anniversary of its opening, it is indeed the opportune time for such a publication.

Rev. Msgr. Ambrose V. Hayden
Pastor
Cathedral of Saint Paul

ACKNOWLEDGMENTS

Like its subject, this book is in varying degrees the product of many knowledgeable and generous contributors. Chief among them is Monsignor Ambrose V. Hayden, current Rector of the Cathedral of Saint Paul. It was Monsignor Hayden's idea to produce a history of the edifice entrusted to his pastoral and administrative care more than twenty-three years ago. In addition to placing the matchless resources of the Cathedral Archives at my disposal, he followed the writing and production process through every stage, offering suggestions which invariably improved both the text and the format. Always a valuable collaborator, he has become a valued friend. An equally strong debt of gratitude, and one equally pleasurable to repay, is owed to Dr. John G. Nemo, Dean of the College of St. Thomas, upon whose recommendation I was commissioned to write this narrative. Through three years of teaching at the College, I found Dr. Nemo consistently supportive. In this literary venture, as in two others, he provided much needed technical and financial assistance.

The staff of the Catholic Historical Society Archives made available to me a number of unpublished materials concerning the four Cathedrals of Saint Paul; at the same time, the reference team at the O'Shaughnessy Library of the College of St. Thomas performed a similar service with respect to hard-to-find published sources. I am indebted to both groups, who met every request for help with impressive expertise and constant congeniality.

This book has also profited from the special contributions of three talented colleagues and good friends: Reverend George Welzbacher, who provided elegant translations of some of the Cathedral's Latin inscriptions; Nancy Giguere, who helped in the decipherment of French manuscripts; and James D. Kellen, who repeatedly and gladly shared his vast knowledge of the Minnesota Catholic experience. With unfailing dedication and efficiency William V. Kirchgessner of the Bureau of Public Affairs, College of St. Thomas, helped expedite the publication process. From beyond the St. Thomas community came the valuable assistance of Professor John Finnegan of the University of Minnesota School of Public Health; Professor Alan K. Lathrop, Curator of the Northwestern Architectural Archives, University of Minnesota; J. Hiram Wilson of the James J. Hill Reference Library, St. Paul; and Alvina O'Brien Hart. In offering additions to or criticisms of the text, they have given to this account more than they realize. A special word of thanks is also extended to the dozens of Minnesotans who, upon hearing of my appointment as historian of the Cathedral, were quick to volunteer personal reminiscences as well as encouragement.

Finally, I should like to express special thanks to the Most Reverend John R. Roach, Archbishop of St. Paul and Minneapolis, for allowing me the opportunity to reconstruct the story of his cathedral.

INTRODUCTION
Structure and Symbol: The Idea of a Cathedral

Defined most simply, a cathedral is a church in which is located a bishop's chair, or *cathedra.* But more than simply a place from which the leader of a diocese celebrates solemn ceremonies, the cathedral is a symbol of his teaching and governing authority. As the bishop's ecclesiastical home, it carries the distinction of being the Mother Church of the area over which that bishop presides.

Though oftentimes the largest and most ornate church in a diocese, a cathedral's canonical status does not depend on its size, style, or degree of decoration. Once it is canonically established — meaning that it is recognized by the Holy See as a bishop's official church — the structure, whether of wood, brick, or stone, whether emphatically splendid or vigorously simple, becomes a cathedral. If its bishop is also a metropolitan, that is, an archbishop enjoying precedence over bishops and dioceses of the surrounding area, a cathedral bears the additional status of metropolitan church. Occasionally, and by special indult of the Holy See, a diocese may have co-cathedrals, each having a permanent episcopal seat; this duality may be allowed for any number of reasons, including Rome's recognition of the need to treat and serve with equal respect two great urban centers within the same diocese. (In the Archdiocese of St. Paul and Minneapolis, for example, the Basilica of St. Mary in Minneapolis serves as the co-cathedral.)

Beyond the nature of the edifice and its canonical distinction, however, is the symbolism of the cathedral. Apart from being the seat of episcopal authority, it is the highest material expression of the faith of its people, a clear sign of what Pope Paul VI spoke of as "the unity of believers." Parish churches undoubtedly hold innumerable memories and thus command undying devotion from their congregations, but only a cathedral can go beyond the parochial, to point to a wider area of spirituality. Every act of adoration, thanksgiving, contrition, and supplication is consciously carried out in the name of, and on behalf of, all the faithful of the diocese, just as in the structure itself every altar, statue, window, and painting is reflective of a wider spirituality than that evinced by those who call the cathedral their parish church. It is to the Mother Church that a new Ordinary comes to be officially installed; within its walls are held a diocese's most solemn liturgies; from its sanctuary come forth the homilies of distinguished ecclesiastical visitors and the first blessings of newly ordained priests.

In short, a cathedral summarizes all that its people are and hope to be. Even in the twentieth century, when, unlike their medieval counterparts, laymen no longer actually participate *en masse* in its construction, it remains a potent symbol of a community of faith, the microcosm of a diocese, a common spiritual home in which "we, many though we are, become one."

"THIS CATHEDRAL WILL, AFTER ALL,
HAVE ITS CHIEF IMPORTANCE,
NOT FROM ITS MASSIVE WALLS,
NOT FROM ITS SKY-POINTED DOMES,
NOT FROM ITS IMPOSING EXTERIOR
OR SPLENDID SETTING, BUT...
FROM THE SPECIAL DISTINCTION
THAT WITHIN IT STANDS
THE TEACHING CHAIR
OF A BISHOP OF GOD'S CHURCH"

Judge William L. Kelly,
Address at the Laying of
the Cornerstone, June 2, 1907.

Overleaf: The Cathedra of the Cathedral of Saint Paul

Chapter One

Conception: The Archbishop and the Architect

Alone and deep in thought, John Ireland sat in the study of his Portland Avenue home. It was March 31, 1904. Earlier that day he had celebrated the Maundy Thursday Mass, his twentieth as Bishop of St. Paul, and sixteenth as Archbishop and Metropolitan of the Province of St. Paul (fig. 1.1). Now, as the last minutes of the day of the Last Supper passed into the first hour of the day of the Crucifixion, he was both delighted and distressed.

The delight came from the obviously "deep devotion of the people," a phenomenon he knew well, and one which never failed to move him.[1] The distress, on the other hand, was born of the equally obvious fact that the forty-six-year-old Cathedral of St. Paul could no longer meet the needs of a growing Archdiocese. It was simply too small, and all too many of the faithful had been forced to stand — some even outside the church — through the solemn and lengthy ceremonies of Holy Week. For all its simple beauty, the structure at Sixth and St. Peter Streets was no longer an adequate symbol of upper Midwestern Catholicism. What was needed, Ireland believed, was a great "Mother Church" which would express the power and durability both of his faith and the faith of his people. After all, he concluded, "Has not the time come for a great Cathedral in St. Paul?"

A Decision Postponed, A Decision Taken

Ireland's momentous decision during the early hours of Good Friday, 1904, was not the first time the idea of a new cathedral had been broached. Soon after the establishment of the Archdiocese and Metropolitanate in 1888, Ireland discussed the possibility of a major construction project with a few friends, including Archbishop John J. Keane of Dubuque.[2] But he had postponed the project at that time, motivated by his belief that the money would be far better spent in support of the recently established Catholic University of America. Preferring teaching to building, Ireland subscribed to the sentiments of a brother Archbishop whom he greatly admired, Cardinal Manning of Westminster: "Could I leave 20,000 children without education, and drain my friends and my flock to pile up stones and bricks?"[3] But through the next two decades the Archbishop of St. Paul kept alive the idea of a "great cathedral" by assembling several large scrapbooks containing photographs, prints, and drawings of the world's most impressive houses of worship. At the same time, he was no doubt stimulated by plans for new cathedrals in Newark, Pittsburgh, Richmond, St. Louis, Omaha, Denver, Seattle, and twenty other American cities.

But by early 1904 Ireland was approaching seventy, and, notwithstanding an incredible energy which earned him the respect of even his opponents, felt that the task of erecting a new Mother Church would be better left to his successor. "I thought that I could allow things to remain as they are and leave the work to a younger bishop," he later told a group of friends. The pragmatic reassessment of Holy Thursday dispelled the cautiousness of age; no longer could he refuse to listen to "...so many...urgent requests from the people for the inauguration of the Cathedral project...."[4] Within ten days, a site, considered the most impressive in all of St. Paul, was scouted, chosen, and purchased. Catholics and non-Catholics alike saw both in the magnificence of the site itself and in the confidence and efficiency with which it was selected, a guarantee that a grand spectacle would be played out over the next few years on the brow of St. Anthony Hill.

The First Archbishop of St. Paul

But then everything about John Ireland was grand. Given their due, his eighty years of accomplishments would fill volumes.[5] Though a central figure in American Catholicism for almost four decades, he played an equally large role in the political and social affairs of his state and country. To every activity and new idea he brought a keen intellect, restless curiosity, intense application, and unconquerable vitality. The same dynamism which inspired his unforgettable preaching, cogent apological writings, and leadership of the temperance movement, underlay his unsuccessful attempt as Vatican representative to mediate the Spanish-American War and his successful efforts to prevent Papal condemnation of the Knights of Labor. For Ireland was convinced that Catholicism, particularly in the modern era, had to reach far beyond the walls of churches. His addresses and essays were rife with references to the need for — and indeed even the duty of — hierarchy and laity alike to manifest the faith in every aspect of their everyday lives:

> We desire to win the age. Let us not, then, stand
> isolated from it. Our place is in the world as well
> as in the sanctuary; in the world, wherever we
> can prove our love for it or render it a service.
> We cannot influence men at close range; close
> contact is needed.[6]

Winning the age for Christianity implied a deep commitment to country and humanity on the part of every Catholic. There was little room in Ireland's Church for apolitical, milquetoast, or indifferent co-religionists. Those who sought the safe and easy way dabbled in "dry-rot."[7] Throughout history, Ireland averred, the Church had shown an abiding concern for every area of life. Beyond the evident spiritual and artistic influences, the

Church had worked aggressively to better material welfare and advance social justice. As an integral part of the American Church's legacy, this devotion to the commonweal demanded a highly visible patriotism, thoroughgoing but not jingoistic, and well-informed. Against those critics who pointed to the "tyranny" of Rome through the ages, this love of country would illustrate a Catholicism committed to the preservation of the liberties of the Republic.[8] "Roman" and "American," far from being exclusive terms, would each hold a valid place in defining the role of Catholics in the United States, a growing body of believers drawn from diverse cultures and yet drawn together by their efforts to reconcile Church and age. "Church and age! They pulsate alike: the God of nature works in one, the God of supernatural revelation works in the other — in both the self-same God....Unite them in the name of humanity, in the name of God."[9]

Ireland's entire episcopal career was spent in the service of "[this] most glorious crusade" of reconciliation. During some thirty-three years as leader of Minnesota's Catholics, he combined what Archbishop Keane called his "twin passions": a religious belief which constituted the essence of his spirit, and a patriotism prompted by the noblest human instincts as well as by Biblical teaching.[10] Celebrated though his Civil War exploits were — he served as chaplain to the Fifth Minnesota Volunteer Infantry — they paled before his activities as Bishop (1884-1888), and later, Archbishop (1888-1918), of St. Paul. He encouraged Catholic immigration to Minnesota, easing the way for homesteaders to settle in rural areas. As the number of Catholics grew, he built schools, hospitals, and charitable institutions. Religion severed from education or humanitarianism, according to Ireland, was not worthy of being labeled "Christian" or "American." To form a strong clergy he established the St. Paul Seminary. To form an alert and intelligent laity, he founded the College of St. Thomas. In 1911 he founded the *Catholic Bulletin,* a weekly designed as much to advertise Catholic progress in the Northwest as to bring together the widely scattered Catholics of his See. Balancing the practical side, however, was Ireland's work as a writer, theologian, and apologist. The thoughtfulness so obvious in his articles, lectures, addresses, and preaching often surprises those familiar only with the man whom Archbishop Ryan of Philadelphia once affectionately dubbed, "the Consecrated Blizzard of the West."[11]

Still, the electricity of the man could not be contained or fully spent within his own archdiocese or province. He played an important role in two key events of late nineteenth-century American Catholicism: the founding of the Catholic University in Washington, D.C.,

1.1 Archbishop John Ireland

and the successful campaign to prevent Papal condemnation of the Knights of Labor. On the international level, he tapped his friendship with Popes, Presidents, and Princes, in the interests of his Church and country. Leo XIII, for whom "the Archbishop of St. Paul [was] a truly great and good man,"[12] sent him as a goodwill ambassador to the notoriously anticlerical republican government of France. Moreover, it was at Ireland's request that President Theodore Roosevelt appointed the Taft Commission to settle the religious problems caused by American acquisition of the Philippines. In all of this Ireland's proclaimed purpose was to show that true faith held as much profit and promise in this life as in the next; immersion in the complex relations of human life was a *sine qua non* of Catholicism.[13] The modern world, as found quintessentially in the American experiment, was to be blessed rather than simply tolerated. Through her doctrine and ministry the Church was to be the "civilizing leaven" in the midst of an increasingly fast-paced and secularized society, and a city on a hill, to which Catholics could look for hope, strength, and pride. In the light of this thinking, Ireland's selection of the cathedral site becomes all the more meaningful.

This eagerness to embrace and sanctify the modern world carried with it at the same time a profound attachment to tradition. Ireland's eight years of seminary training in France, at Meximieux and Montbel, filled him with admiration for the splendors of medieval and Renaissance Christendom; this most "modern" of American prelates was always enraptured by the sight of a great European church. They were enterprises which he knew had been possible only through the collaboration of a dynamic bishop, talented architects, and a pious and generous laity. But it was not primarily the size, beauty, or cost of these cathedrals which excited Ireland. Rather, it was their symbolism: "They were truly monuments of faith and piety, and more eloquently than the most eloquent pages of written history they tell us that in older times the children of the Church were giants in devotion to religion."[14] Expressions of Christian vitality, they were the most impressive symbols of a faith which had edified almost two thousand years of Western civilization. Given this perspective, as well as the personality of John Ireland,

1.2 Emmanuel Louis Masqueray

it would have been relatively easy for many Minnesota Catholics to accurately gauge the scope of the plan formulated by their Archbishop late on the evening of Holy Thursday, 1904. The choice of architect would have indeed confirmed their prediction.

A Parisian on the Prairie

Probably no architect was better able to translate John Ireland's vision into stone than Emmanuel Louis Masqueray (fig. 1.2). As the Archbishop wrote, before the completion of the Cathedral: "Masqueray caught up at once in his fancy the full significance of the great Christian temple, and, as it were, with magic pencil set himself to portray in stone the splendid picture of religion's meaning, religion's history, religion's purposes."[15] For the historically minded Ireland the relationship was quite consciously a re-creation of that cooperation of prelate and artist which had graced the cities of Western and Southern Europe with great cathedrals. For Masqueray, who shared a passion for the Middle Ages and who consistently underscored the personal nature of the collaboration by signing his letters to the Archbishop, "*Your* Architect," the years with Ireland yielded a score of commissions throughout the Northwest, with the Cathedral of St. Paul as their masterpiece.[16]

Ireland accurately described his architect as "the chosen child of art — the child of art in every throbbing of soul, in every pencilling of finger."[17] Though born in Dieppe, France, on September 10, 1861, Masqueray was raised in the city of Rouen, where playing among such architectural masterpieces as the Cathedral of Notre-Dame, the churches of St-Maclou and St-Ouen, and the Hôtel de Ville, formed his earliest memories. His interest in architecture, encouraged by his parents, deepened after the family relocated to Paris in 1873. In 1879, at the age of seventeen, he entered the Ecole des Beaux-Arts, the oldest and most prestigious fine arts school in the world. There he quickly established a reputation for both academic excellence and artistic talent. Had he not decided early that he would spend no more time at the school than absolutely necessary, he would have certainly won the *Prix de Rome,* the most important of all the awards given by the Ecole des Beaux-Arts during the nineteenth century. Other honors did, however, come along during the course of his studies: the *Prix Deschaumes* of the Institut de France (1880) and the *Prix Chaudesaigues* (1881), which financed a trip to Italy, at that time a requisite for all serious students of design.

Masqueray's two years in Italy gave him first-hand knowledge of the architectural principles he had learned in Paris. His education at the Ecole des Beaux-Arts had been far-reaching. Under the influence of Charles-Jean

Laisné, his first instructor, he had refined his love of that medieval and Renaissance architecture which formed part of his earliest memories of Rouen. Laisné's successor, Paul-René Léon Ginain, on the other hand, had exposed him to the Néo- Grec style, which emphasized the primacy of decoration in producing a design. By the time he departed for Italy, Masqueray was set in his dedication to a historically minded, highly intellectual architecture. In this, the criteria for proper design were the same as those used by the French philosophical eclectics earlier in the century to test the validity of an idea: truth, beauty, and goodness. While the latter two, according to the Beaux-Arts tradition, were achieved by following that classical style so familiar and acceptable to the public, the first demanded not only that a design take into account the vagaries of location and climate, but also, and more importantly, that the exterior of a building clearly reflect the purpose for which it was constructed.[18] Finally, once having achieved its desired state, a design should never be altered; Ireland was no doubt echoing Masqueray's sentiments in this regard when he noted, shortly before the completion of the Cathedral, "Were plans for the Cathedral to be wrought anew today, not one line, not one elevation, not one chapel, not one curve in vaulting or ambulatory should we dare alter."[19] Given this creed, it is small wonder that Masqueray devoted most of his Italian visit to the study of Renaissance architecture, with its purity of design and aura of timelessness.

Upon returning to Paris in 1883 Masqueray was awarded a gold medal at the annual Salon for his drawings of the then little-known Ducal Palace at Urbino, one of the greatest products of fifteenth-century Italy. Succeeding salons hosted his renditions of Roman and French sites, the latter of which were bought by the Minister of Fine Arts for the Commission des Monuments historiques. In 1886, and on the strength of his drawings, Masqueray was appointed to the ecclesiastical department of the Commission. However, few of his proposals for the reconstruction of timeworn cathedrals were implemented, since he remained in his position for less than a year.

In 1887 Masqueray was invited by John M. Carrère, a former classmate at the Beaux-Arts, to join the fledgling architectural firm of Carrère and Hastings in New York. Five years later he resigned what seemed to be a dead-end position, becoming "chief assistant" to Richard Morris Hunt, the first American graduate of the Beaux-Arts and one of the leading American architects of the period. During his five years with the Hunt studio, Masqueray established and operated his own school. Modeled closely after the Beaux- Arts, for which it served as a preparatory institute, the Atelier Masqueray has been called the first

modern example of architectural training in the United States.[20] By 1897, the year in which Masqueray left the Hunt office and joined the firm of Warren and Westmore, the school had graduated eighty-one students. Through his four apparently happy years with Warren and Westmore, his reputation continued to grow. It therefore came as no surprise to the American architectural community when, in July 1901, he was chosen as chief of design for the Louisiana Purchase Exposition to be held in St. Louis. Forced by the planners to work exclusively in that Neo-Baroque style so castigated by all faithful sons of the Beaux-Arts, Masqueray devised several ingenious designs, including those for the Transportation, Agricultural, Horticultural, Fish and Game, and Forestry Palaces, the Colonnade of States, and the Louisiana Purchase Monument. Also from his drawing-board came the designs for the Exposition's bridges, bandstands, statuary, decorative pavilions, landscaping, and the overall siting of the buildings. His work was on the whole well-received. Delighted fairgoers could not have suspected how distressing this devotee of simple and rational architecture found his own creations.

Yet the almost three years of work in St. Louis were not a complete loss. Soon after the opening of the Exposition in May 1904, Masqueray was introduced to an important ecclesiastical visitor, the Archbishop of St. Paul, who, in his eagerness for things modern, had come for a visit. Masqueray immediately took to the French-trained prelate whose visionary and energetic personality was very much like his own. For his part, Ireland was greatly impressed both by the architecture of the Fair and its creator, to whom he mentioned his recent decision to construct a great metropolitan cathedral. He invited Masqueray to visit St. Paul, hoping that the architect might settle there permanently.[21] Early in 1905, the Frenchman opened an office in the Dispatch Building. In locating and attracting an architect at once deeply Catholic and highly creative, Ireland had brought his dream of Holy Thursday evening one step closer to reality.

Chapter Two

Anticipation: The Earlier Structures

Overleaf: **Our Lady of Victory** (Cathedral Museum)
Brought from France by Bishop Cretin in 1851, this statue stood in both the second and third Cathedrals. It is a somewhat smaller version of an image honored for centuries in the Church of Notre-Dame-des-Victoires, Paris.

The majesty of the structure on St. Anthony Hill often obscures the fact that it is the fourth building to bear the name "Cathedral of St. Paul." Though smaller in size and simpler in design, each of its three predecessors reflected the changing status and increasingly higher aspirations of the first three generations of Minnesota Catholics. If Ireland's monument expressed that triumphalism so integral a part of the early twentieth-century American Church, the modest edifices of Galtier, Cretin, Ravoux, and Grace bespoke the devotion, energy, and hard work without which that later sense of optimism and assertiveness would have been impossible.

The Chapel on the Bluff

Those familiar with today's Cathedral of St. Paul would no doubt find its first incarnation far from prepossessing. In the spring of 1840 the newly ordained Father Lucien Galtier (fig. 2.1) was sent to the settlement of Pig's Eye by Bishop Mathias Loras of Dubuque. His instructions were to minister to the French Canadians who had recently settled there, after their forced removal by American soldiers from homes in the Fort Snelling-Mendota area.

2.1 Father Lucien Galtier

Needing a chapel, Galtier scouted three sites. Only one of these, on a bluff, one hundred feet above the river, and easily accessible by land and water, appealed to him. In mid-1841 Vital Guerin and Benjamin Gervais, "two good, quiet farmers" and the owners of the land, donated a section large enough to accommodate a church, garden, and cemetery.

Construction of the chapel was completed within the month of October 1841. Eight volunteers were responsible for most of the work on the log structure: Joseph Labissonniere, who served as general superintendent; Isaac Labissonniere, his son; the two Pierre Gervais; Pierre and Charles Bottineau; François Morin; and Vital Guerin, former owner of the site. As the building neared completion, other settlers offered their services. Nearly seven decades later, Isaac Labissonniere, who was eighteen years old when the chapel was built, recalled the hardships of construction and their mitigation by the generosity and commitment of the local Catholic community:

> The ground selected for the site of the church was thinly covered with groves of red oak and white oak. Where the cathedral stands was then a tamarack swamp. The logs for the chapel were cut on the spot, and the tamarack swamp in the rear was made to contribute rafters and roof pieces. We had poor building tools in those days, and our work was not beautifully finished. The logs, rough and undressed, prepared merely by the ax, were made secure by wooden pins. The roof was made of steeply slanting bark-covered slabs, donated by a millowner of Stillwater. The slabs were carried to St. Paul by a steamboat, the captain accepting in payment a few days' service of one of the men. These slabs were landed at Jackson street, and were drawn up the hill by hand with ropes. The slabs were likewise put to good use in the construction of the floor and of the benches.
>
> The chapel, as I remember it, was about twenty-five feet long, eighteen feet wide, and ten feet high. It had a single window on each side and it faced the river. It was completed in a few days, and could not have represented an expenditure in labor value of more than $65.[1]

On the Feast of All Saints, November 1, 1841, Galtier dedicated the new chapel, which, with its unshaven sides, barksided roof, and surrounding area of trees and tangled growth, reminded him of the stable of Bethlehem.[2] He placed the building and its community under the patronage of St. Paul, hoping from the first that the saint's name might someday grace not only his chapel but the entire Pig's Eye settlement. In a letter of 1864 to Bishop

Grace, the aging Galtier justified his original selection of a patron saint and outlined his determined (and ultimately successful) efforts to realize his hope:

> The church was dedicated to St. Paul, and I expressed a wish that the settlement should be known by no other name. I succeeded in this. I had previously to this time fixed my residence at St. Peter [i.e., Mendota], and as the name of St. Paul is generally connected with that of St. Peter, and the Gentiles being well represented in the new place in the persons of Indians, I called it St. Paul's....
>
> The name of St. Paul, applied to a town or city, seemed appropriate. The monosyllable is short, sounds well, is understood by all denominations. Hence, when later an attempt was made to change the name of the place, I opposed the vain project, even by writing from Prairie du Chien. When Mr. Vital [Guerin] was married, I published the banns as being those of a resident of St. Paul. An American named Jackson put up a store, and a grocery was opened at the foot of the Gervais claim. This soon caused steamboats to land there; henceforward the place was known as St. Paul landing.[3]

Following Galtier's transfer to Iowa in 1844, the chapel and its congregation were placed under the direction of Father Augustine Ravoux (fig. 2.2). Finding the building too small for the needs of his growing community, Ravoux enlarged it in 1847, adding to the rear of the structure an area just slightly smaller than that covered by the original chapel (fig. 2.3). Joined together, the old and new fabrics — with the former shingled and repaired so as to harmonize with the latter — measured forty-five by eighteen feet.[4] During the winter of 1847-1848, Ravoux constructed a small belfry beside the chapel, to house the bell of the *Argo,* a steamer which had sunk in the Mississippi a few months earlier. It was to this revised and somewhat refurbished chapel that Joseph Cretin came in July 1851, to be installed as first Bishop of St. Paul (fig. 2.4).

During its first ten years, the chapel of St. Paul was not a cathedral; it held no *cathedra,* or bishop's chair, and received only one episcopal visitation, when in 1842 Bishop Loras administered confirmation within its sanctuary. It was the decision of the Seventh Provincial Council of Baltimore, held in 1849, to erect a new ecclesiastical jurisdiction in the northern part of the Diocese of Dubuque, which changed the status of the modest chapel on the Mississippi bluff. A year after the official establishment of the Diocese of St. Paul, on July 2, 1851, the log chapel was formally proclaimed the Cathedral of St. Paul.

2.2 Father Augustine Ravoux

Bishop Cretin and the Second Cathedral

But it was clear that the new Cathedral would not enjoy its status and solemn ceremonies for long. During his installation, Cretin was disturbed by the large numbers of the faithful forced to stand outside. A log chapel forty-five by eighteen feet might have been suitable for a few hundred souls, but the population of the nascent Diocese was now approximately three thousand, and growing. Cretin soon discovered that even before his arrival in St. Paul, Ravoux had bought land for a new cathedral. The seller was Vital Guerin, who had donated the site for the log chapel a decade earlier. Within five months of Cretin's installation, the new cathedral was completed, dedicated, and in use.[5] Total cost of the project, including the land acquisition, was $5,900.

Located in the center of the burgeoning downtown district, at the corner of Sixth and Wabasha Streets, the brick structure measured eighty-four by forty-four feet and featured three stories (fig. 2.5). The three-aisled church was on the second floor. The top floor included living and working quarters for the Bishop, his seminarians, and the Brothers of the Holy Family who had accompanied Cretin to the United States. The first floor contained a library, kitchen, parlor, and dining, school, and store rooms.[6] But almost from its day of dedication it was hopelessly cramped, due to the large variety of uses to which it was put. Thus was destroyed Cretin's ideal of a compact structure which could effectively fill a large number of needs. The close juxtaposition of sacred and secular pursuits within the building frequently had disconcerting results. As Father Anatole Oster, one of the seminarian residents of the third floor, remembered:

> On more than one occasion the furnace in the kitchen was the cause of considerable amusement. The pipe from its hot-air chamber opened into the Sanctuary not far from the Bishop's throne, and through it the sounds and odors from the kitchen were occasionally conveyed to the worshipers. One Christmas eve the solemnity of the pontifical midnight Mass was interrupted by the vigorous grinding of coffee and I was dispatched in haste to put an end to the performance. At another time, during the High Mass, the air pipe began to send forth a dark column of smoke from the roast which the cook had placed in the hot air chamber and forgotten. When the Bishop realized the state of affairs he dexterously kicked the cushion under his feet so that it landed on the opening and prevented further annoyance.[7]

Bishop Grace and the Third Cathedral

While Cretin was prepared to tolerate the unpredic-tability and inconvenience of life in his Cathedral, he could not ignore the fact that both the Catholic population and diocesan administration were outgrowing the spaces allotted to them on the upper two floors of the building. As early as 1853 he initiated plans for a third cathedral, not only larger than its predecessor but deliberately reflective of the increasing prestige and prosperity of the Catholic community. Advertised widely as the most impressive religious structure west of Chicago,[8] it would be built of stone, measure one hundred and seventy- five by one hundred feet, and boast a steeple two hundred and fifty feet high. To strengthen and relieve the monotony of the lateral walls a series of buttresses would be added.

Work began at the site on the corner of St. Peter and Sixth Streets in July 1854. With the foundation sufficiently advanced, the cornerstone was solemnly laid in place on July 27, 1856. Ireland noted many years later that "Bishop Cretin was radiant with joy: his dream of great things to be done in his diocese was taking visible form....The day closed in gladsome hopes that the work would be done quickly and well."[9] These hopes were soon destroyed, for less than a year later Cretin died, and the financial panic of 1857 followed. All work on the building stopped.

With characteristic determination, Ravoux, after being named diocesan administrator in July 1858, com-

2.3 The Log Chapel of Saint Paul, with addition, 1847

pleted the project, but with modifications. Due to lack of funds, he excised all architectural ornamentation from the original design, including the buttresses and steeple. What remained was a solid, spacious, and inexpensive structure (fig. 2.6), in which the first Mass was celebrated on June 13, 1858.[10] Work on the interior continued into early 1860, by which time the total cost of building the third Cathedral was set at $33,647.94. Of this total, $18,987.59 had been provided by the French Society for the Propagation of the Faith. Not long after his own installation in the new Cathedral, on July 29, 1859, Thomas Langdon Grace (fig. 2.7), Cretin's successor, added transepts to the rear of the building, partly to strengthen as well as artistically enliven the main walls, and partly to deal with a problem all too familiar to his predecessors, Ravoux and Cretin: too little space for an increasingly larger number of worshipers.[11] Grace foresaw the need for yet another and even larger Cathedral. In fact, on one occasion he showed his coadjutor, John Ireland, a most appropriate new site: the brow of St. Anthony Hill.[12]

Grace's resignation as Bishop of St. Paul on July 31, 1884, meant that the challenge and vision of a new Cathedral passed to John Ireland.

2.5 The Second Cathedral of Saint Paul

2.4 Bishop Joseph Cretin

14

2.6 The Third Cathedral of Saint Paul

2.7 Bishop Thomas Langdon Grace

Chapter Three

Birth: A Great Church for a Great City

Overleaf: ***The Metropolitan Processional Cross of Archbishop John Ireland*** (Cathedral Museum)

Having reached his decision to build a great cathedral, Ireland set out to execute it with a verve and efficiency which surprised even his closest associates. Through his forceful personality and prestige as Archbishop of St. Paul, every obstacle — physical, financial, and psychological — seemed to melt, giving way to ten years of uninterrupted building, fund-gathering, and popular optimism.

The Question of Location

There had been no dearth of proposals for the cathedral site during Ireland's first two decades as Ordinary. In evaluating each proposed location, the Archbishop applied three key criteria:

> It should be in a permanent locality, it should be in a section of the city removed from any possibility of ever becoming a business section, and it should be in the direction of Minneapolis, for the Bishop of St. Paul is at the same time the spiritual chief of our neighboring city, and the Cathedral is a church, which in a certain sense, belongs to the Catholics of all the diocese and should be consequently situated as conveniently to the homes of the largest number of them as possible.[1]

By the late 1880s Ireland began to feel that these criteria could be fulfilled only in the Midway District, an area growing in population and prominence. He believed that the Twin Cities would soon merge into one great urban conglomerate called "Paulopolis," and that the Midway, the projected home of the new State Capitol and Union Depot, would become its political and economic center, "the very heart of the coming great city."[2] Furthermore, such a location was close to the projected St. Paul Seminary and the College of St. Thomas, where for some time Ireland had planned to build the archiepiscopal residence.[3] No land, however, was ever acquired, for Ireland's vision of a single "federal city" soon crumbled, leaving him to realize that, progress in the Midway notwithstanding, "a Cathedral..., equidistant between the cities, would be a Cathedral in the country."[4] With the abandonment of the Midway design, other sites were rumored as being in Ireland's sights, including the Wann property on Summit Avenue and Victoria Street, and the corner of Western and St. Anthony Avenues, both of which the Diocese already owned.

Ireland's decision of Holy Thursday, 1904, made the choice of a site imperative. If he had forgotten Bishop Grace's recommendation of the Kittson land on St. Anthony Hill,[5] it had been brought back to him in 1903, when two prominent St. Paul businessmen, Charles H.F. Smith and A.B. Stickney, offered to purchase the site for the archiepiscopal residence.[6] He had rejected their proposal to collect the necessary $50,000 from fifty well-to-do Minnesota Catholics, arguing diocesan financial inability to build the structure and the likelihood of adverse public response to a bishop's house in so prominent a place. But a site too grand for a churchman's home was singularly appropriate for a Divine residence. Ireland's decision to obtain the land was made a day or two after his decision to build the Cathedral.

At this point events moved so rapidly that there is some confusion about their exact sequence. Adding to the historian's frustration in attempting to provide an accurate reconstruction of events, is the absence of any official record of the earliest initiatives. Nevertheless, much can be clarified by referring to the correspondence and personal reminiscences of the leading figures in the enterprise.

On April 5, 1904, a mere five days after he had made his decision, Ireland met with Smith and H.C. McNair at the Archbishop's residence. There he told them of his plan for a monumental structure costing a million dollars, on the site bordered by Summit, Selby, and Dayton Avenues. Smith and McNair were elated and assured the Archbishop that the sum could be collected within a five-year period. Although Ireland, according to Smith, "seemed to doubt [that] such a sum could be collected in that space of time," he finally deferred to the expertise of the two financiers and authorized them to purchase the Kittson plot, but for no more than $60,000.[7] Four days later, on April 9, Smith obtained the land, with its ornate but run-down Victorian mansion, for $52,000 (fig. 3.1). To protect the sale, Smith provided a down-payment of $2,000 of his own money.[8] So quickly had the deal been made that even Ireland was amazed. The day after the sale, Smith brought the deed to the Archbishop's house. Ireland believed that the speed of the transaction was a sign: "The hand of God is in it."[9] Divine approval was complemented by the apparently unanimous endorsement of the Catholics of the Twin Cities. As Ireland noted many years later, "Seldom has an act of mine received such universal approval as the selection of that site."[10] Shortly after the purchase, Francesco Cardinal Satolli, Apostolic Delegate to the United States, visited St. Paul and gave the entire effort the much-welcomed sign of Roman favor.[11]

The Formation of Committees

The necessary committees formed rapidly. On July 15, Ireland wrote a letter to a number of leading laymen, requesting that they serve on a Board of Consultors:

3.1 The Kittson Mansion, c. 1895 Built in 1875 by Commodore Norman W. Kittson, a wealthy merchant and prominent civic leader, this elaborate Victorian piece was one of the most beautiful homes in the city. In 1895, following years of neglect brought about by the breakup of the Kittson family, it was sold to the St. Paul Title and Trust Company, from which the Diocese would purchase it some nine years later.

In my attempt to build a Cathedral worthy of the City of St. Paul and the Diocese of St. Paul, I need wise counsel and active co-operation; and, for this reason, I have decided to associate with myself a number of intelligent and zealous Catholic laymen, who, understanding the importance of the task upon which I am entering, will not be unwilling to share with me the labor and responsibility which it imposes. It will be a very great pleasure for me to have you as one of my co-workers; and I respectfully ask that I be permitted to name you a member of my Board of Consultors.

As the building of a Cathedral is an enterprise of the whole Diocese, I am inviting to membership in the Board of Consultors representative Catholics from all parishes of the City — not merely from those that will derive more immediate profit from the new edifice.[12]

Meanwhile, behind the scenes Smith made sure that all those invited to be Board members would accept the summons. On July 24 he hosted an informal gathering at his home on Summit Avenue, not far from the construction site.[13] At this meeting he presented the Archbishop's vision to his guests, who responded with promises of financial as well as personal support. At the first official meeting of the Board of Consultors, held on July 28 at

Raudenbush Hall, two hundred and five laymen and almost one hundred priests joined in what Ireland dubbed "the initiatory step towards the realization of the great project."[14] An enthusiastic audience heard its Archbishop speak of the history of the previous cathedrals, the pressing need for a new one, and the importance of completing it within five years. Short responses were proffered by representatives of the Board, including A.L. Larpenteur, who had been appointed by Bishop Cretin to the committee for the construction of the third cathedral. Before the end of the session Smith moved that the Archbishop be empowered to appoint an executive committee of nine, to deal with the day-to-day business of construction. The motion was carried unanimously.[15]

Expanded to include twelve laymen and six clergymen, the Executive Building Committee met for the first time on September 28, 1904 (fig. 3.2).[16] Ireland was elected President, with Louis W. Hill as Treasurer and John B. Meagher as Secretary. Smith was named Chairman of the Sub-committee on Finance. That the group's second and third meetings, on October 8 and 17, were concerned solely with finances, including the crucial issue of how to word the subscriber's pledge, demonstrated the group's practical outlook.

It was not until the Executive Building Committee's fourth meeting that the issue of selecting an architect was raised. On December 29, the Committee decided to hold an architectural competition, "limited or mixed," with Glenn Brown, Secretary of the American Institute of Architects, as the Committee's adviser. A Sub-committee on Plans, composed of Christopher D. O'Brien, Thomas Fitzpatrick, and John S. Grode, would screen and sort the different designs for consideration by the entire committee.[17] From the first, Committee members stipulated that the design had to be "of Renaissance style, with a modern dome, i.e., a broader curve and shallower in depth, like the Festival Hall at St. Louis and the Hall of Fame in New York."[18]

Selection of an Architect

Eleven well-established firms were invited to join the competition. All agreed. Eight of the firms were headquartered in New York: Cram, Goodhue and Ferguson; Heins and LaFarge; Delano and Aldrich; Joseph H.

McGuire; Carrère and Hastings; George B. Post and Sons; McKim, Mead and White; and E.L. Masqueray. The other three were Maginnis, Walsh and Sullivan of Boston; F.W. Fitzpatrick of Washington, D.C.; and Egan and Prindeville of Chicago.[19] Suddenly, however, Ireland scuttled the competition. The Archbishop asked Brown in early February 1905 to limit his inquiries to only four of the original eleven candidates: Delano and Aldrich; McGuire; Maginnis, Walsh and Sullivan; and Masqueray. Though Brown vouched for the competence of all four, his investigation by this time was futile. In reading the Ireland-Brown correspondence, it is clear that Ireland favored Masqueray. By early March, only the Frenchman had become the focus of their dialogue. Brown, however, did not share Ireland's unqualified admiration for the designer of the Louisiana Purchase Exposition:

Mr. E.L. Masqueray, I understand, graduated at

3.2 The Executive Building Committee *Top, left to right:* Jeremiah C. Kennedy, Father F.X. Bajec, Francis M. Erling, Father Patrick R. Heffron, Father John M. Solnce. *Middle, left to right:* George N. Gerlach, Father John J. Lawler, Peter M. Kerst, John S. Grode, Father Thomas J. Gibbons. *Bottom, left to right:* Judge Edward W. Bazille, Charles H.F. Smith, Archbishop John Ireland, Timothy Foley, H.C. McNair, Christopher D. O'Brien.

the Ecole des Beaux-Arts, Paris, France, after which he entered for the Prix de Rome, taking one of the prizes but not gaining the grand prize. He established an atelier in New York and the work of his pupils show [sic] the effect of excellent teaching.

His work as a designer in modern French Renaissance is considered of a high quality; personally, I am inclined more to the Italian Renaissance. He has worked for others in the French style very satisfactorily, showing high artistic qualities. In the management of an office or the conduct of work on his own account I cannot find that he has done any thing noteworthy.[20]

Brown's lukewarm endorsement did not seem to bother Ireland. A few perceptive observers were aware of his favoring Masqueray even before the announcement of the competition. F.W. Fitzpatrick, one of the original competitors, had visited St. Paul in late January 1905. His meeting with Ireland, he later told Christopher D. O'Brien, Chairman of the Sub-committee on Plans, gave him the rather unmistakable feeling that the Archbishop had already chosen his architect. "Had I supposed for a moment that the field was open to me too," Fitzpatrick concluded, "I should certainly not have gone in [a] roundabout way to call attention to myself."[21]

Fitzpatrick's reading of the Archbishop's mind was quite accurate. Setting aside the competition, without at first informing the architects initially solicited, the Committee moved on March 7 to invite Masqueray to St. Paul for an interview. Less than two weeks later, on March 20, Ireland informed Masqueray of his selection as architect of the Cathedral of St. Paul. Acknowledging "the receit [sic] of your letter of the 20th st [sic] with enclosed contract," Masqueray shared with his new boss his happiness over receiving so many congratulations from all quarters, and especially from his "concurrents," i.e., his professional peers.[22] Some of these same "concurrents," incidentally, were quick to congratulate Ireland and the Committee on their choice. Such a demarche on their part was exceptionally admirable, since the announcement of Masqueray's selection was their first notification that the anticipated competition had been set aside some two weeks earlier. Though disappointed at being passed over "because I had sufficient confidence in my own ability to have hoped that the result might have been favorable to me upon competitive plans," Joseph H. McGuire hailed Masqueray as "a distinguished and respected member of the profession...[whose]...efforts will result in a monumental building that will be a credit to your Diocese, your

Committee, and himself."[23] Proud of their former employee, John M. Carrère and Thomas Hastings wrote that they could not find words sincere enough to express their joy.[24]

Why Masqueray?
Congratulations by "good losers" aside, one question remained: Why had the competition been abandoned? What had occurred between December 29, 1904, and March 7, 1905? The Committee's shift was most likely a combination of two realizations. Apparently Ireland and his associates had been convinced by the architectural community that the competitive method would not necessarily yield the most qualified designer. Moreover, many believed that pitting one architect against another degraded the entire profession. In their congratulatory letter, Carrère and Hastings referred to their earlier efforts to change the Committee's *modus operandi:*

> We cannot congratulate you too sincerely on the very wise conclusion which you have reached both as to the method of procedure by direct appointment and as to the selection which you have made by the appointment of Mr. Masqueray. Much as we should like to have become your architects for this great work, we congratulate ourselves that there is to be no competition, and if we have in the slightest degree assisted you in arriving at this conclusion we shall feel that we have done our duty to our profession, to you and to ourselves, and we shall also feel that you have established a precedent which will have much beneficial influence in helping to place future work of this character and importance directly in the hands of competent artists selected for their established merit and their recognized fitness to deal with the problem, rather than by the unsatisfactory, inconclusive and haphazard method of a competition. We realize that it has required considerable courage to depart from the popular method of selecting an architect and we congratulate you, and we are convinced that the result will justify your conclusions in every possible way.[25]

A second and far more important consideration, however, was that a contest measured the advantages of design, but not the personality of the designer. Ireland's collaborator would have to be a very special individual, one whose personal qualities mattered as much as his artistic talent. After only one meeting with the Archbishop of St. Paul, the percipient F.W. Fitzpatrick sketched the extraordinary perspective and abilities required of the new Cathedral's architect:

> ...with Archbishop Ireland it is as with the

prelates of old, the abbots and bishops who to all intents and purposes built their own grand cathedrals and abbeys, caring for every detail and making these monuments parts of their very lives and certainly superb examples of the art of the time. Yet in every case, or at least almost every case, were those prelates aided by laymen versed in architecture and technical experts....Whoever is selected certainly has a big problem ahead of him.

He must put his whole heart and talent into its solution, he must approach that task reverently and with poetic feeling, realizing that the Cathedral must typify a faith that fundamentally has stood the shock of ages, unchanging and unchangeable; the building must be founded on some style or scheme hallowed by churchly precedents — though it need not slavishly follow every twisting and turning of some special style — yet, like the faith, it must be suited to our modern needs, thoughts and modes of expression. You must realize that this Cathedral is in the new world and to be built in the twentieth century, and while it may have the flavor, so to speak, of antiquity, it must at the same time be to all intents and purposes a modern building, perfect in its acoustics, in its sanitary, ventilating, heating and other details, and too, you must remember, in past ages, labor was that of love if not indeed almost slavery, while today you are confronted with labor at so many dollars per day, which is absolutely prohibitive of the ornamentation lavished upon cathedrals of medieval times.

[The] architect must first and foremost be an artist but he must also be an intensely practical man; he must be well equipped with experience and must know men and markets and materials on the tips of his fingers, and be ready to avail himself of every advantage that will redound to the benefit of the work in hand. He must buy materials on low markets and use labor when other works are lying idle. He must instill the sentiment, and reverence and dignity, and grandeur one naturally expects in an ecclesiastical monument, but he must do it with cunningly modern hands or he will swamp your society with expense. He must not start out, as in the case of your Capitol, with a promised expenditure of a million and a quarter, and wind up with four millions and a half! You must confide in him, trust him, but also realize that he is but human, therefore you must not place the temptation in his way of a commission that increases as the cost of a building grows.[26]

While Ireland and the Committee could not be certain that Masqueray's competitors could fulfill these exacting criteria, they were convinced, given the Archbishop's favorable impression from St. Louis and its validation during the interview in St. Paul, that Masqueray could. Was he not, after all, the only architect among the initial eleven to agree to enter the competition without qualification?[27] Moreover, bolstering his cooperative nature were his lifelong devotion to the Catholic Church and his thoroughgoing commitment to the construction of a great temple on the prairie.

Shortly after presenting initial sketches to the Executive Building Committee on June 1, 1905, Masqueray set out on a four-month tour of the great French cathedrals, to look for ideas. While in France, he completed the working plans, eagerly showing them to Archbishop Fuzet of Rouen, who noted in a letter to Ireland that many of the aesthetic elements of his own Cathedral on the banks of the Seine would reappear in the new Cathedral on the banks of the Mississippi.[28] Returning to St. Paul on November 15, 1905, Masqueray presented his drawings at an Executive Building Committee meeting the same day. The Committee accepted them immediately.

Masqueray's Vision
Masqueray proposed to create a grand and serene edifice which would also be representative of the democratic, fast-paced society in which it was located. The design called for a modified Renaissance style, twentieth-century in its purpose and ambience, but medieval in many of its secondary features, including the chapels and organ gallery. Like Michelangelo's original design for St. Peter's in Rome, Masqueray's plan was in the form of a Greek cross with nearly equal arms and with ambulatories and aisles separating the main body of the church from a number of surrounding chapels (fig. 3.3).[29] Yet to create a quintessentially modern structure, the transepts would be wider, and the nave shorter than those found in medieval and Renaissance designs. Over the crossing of nave and transepts rose an out-of-scale dome, "the feature of the composition," reminiscent of the twelfth-century Cathedral of St-Front in Périgueux, and the late nineteenth-century Basilica of Sacré-Coeur-de-Montmartre, in Paris.[30] The three front entrances rested under a monumental arch, which also framed a large rose window (fig. 3.4). Immediately inside the entrances was a vestibule, flanked by a Founders' Chapel and a baptistry, each surmounted by a tower.

Like the Archbishop whose church it was to be, everything about the interior design was grand (fig. 3.5). The main nave measured sixty feet in width and eighty-four in height; twelve-foot-wide ambulatories on each

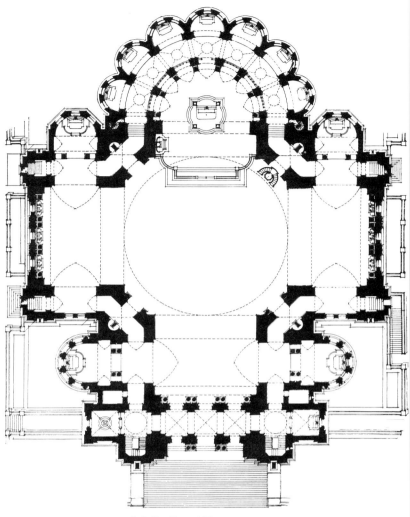

3.3 The Ground Plan (Masqueray)

side of the nave gave access to the chapels of the Blessed Virgin and St. Joseph. Of the same dimensions as the nave, the transepts ended in chapels to be dedicated to St. Peter and St. Paul. The sanctuary, measuring sixty-five by sixty feet, occupied the entire apse. Behind it, yet separated by marble-columned arches, radiated six chapels, to honor the apostles of the nations whose sons and daughters had settled the Northwest. Crowning the entire composition was the great dome, ninety-six feet in diameter and one hundred and seventy-five feet in inner height (figs. 3.6, 3.7). Within this splendid ensemble could be accommodated 2,500 worshipers in the pews, and 3,500 by the addition of removable chairs (fig. 3.8).

So immense a structure might have seemed too impractical an everyday center of worship, yet Masqueray averred that his major preoccupation was to compose an edifice in which "the principal object was that the congregation could see and hear."[31] Consequently, he designed the interior to be completely open, providing from every part a clear view both of the altar and the pulpit, while simultaneously stimulating religious feeling through the picturesque grouping of secondary architectural features such as the ambulatories, chapels, and organ loft. To assure the degree of lighting conducive to proper worship,

Masqueray placed twenty-four large windows at the base of the dome, to flood the sanctuary with light. Rose windows in the transepts would join their counterpart in the facade to provide the same effect in the pews. The overall result would be an edifice stunning yet practical, dramatic yet controlled, lofty yet earth-bound.

The majesty of the design would be equally clear in the exterior. The dimensions were enormous: two hundred and seventy-four feet in length and two hundred and fourteen feet in width. The main facade measured one hundred and thirty by one hundred and forty feet, while its twin towers reached a height of one hundred and fifty feet. The dome, some one hundred and twenty feet wide, peaked at two hundred and eighty feet. True to the principles he had learned at the Ecole des Beaux-Arts, Masqueray conceived the exterior as "the frank architectural expression of the interior,...distinguished by broad treatment of wall surfaces and dignity of proportions...."[32] Such broad treatment and dignity led him to group ornamentation at certain points rather than to disperse it liberally over the entire surface, as he had been required to do in his designs for the Louisiana Purchase Exposition. In addition to maximizing the visual effect of the ornamentation, this grouping would emphasize the key

3.4 The Front Elevation (Masqueray)

elements of the entire design — the facade, towers, sides, entrances, and dome. Framing this ensemble was a series of spacious ramps and walks. Not only would these provide an artistic setting for the building; they would guarantee easy access to all seven entrances, with a minimum of congregational logjam. As with every other aspect of Masqueray's enterprise, building for the glory of God did not mean ignoring human convenience. The sacred and the secular were thus blended in stone.

The Campaign for Funds

But that stone, and all else that Masqueray envisioned as comprising his great cathedral, would involve a great deal of money. Even before Masqueray's appointment, Ireland

had estimated that the project would cost some one million dollars.[33] The Executive Building Committee had inaugurated a campaign for subscriptions at its second meeting (October 8, 1904), more than two months before its initial deliberations over the selection of an architect. Priests and laymen were tapped as solicitors throughout the Archdiocese; blank forms, pledging monthly installments payable to Louis W. Hill, Treasurer of the Executive Building Committee, were consigned to all the parishes.[34] Among the first subscribers were the Foley Brothers, who donated $40,000, and Hill and Smith, each of whom gave $20,000. By November 15, 1905, $347,427 had been pledged, with another $20,625 received in cash. At the

3.5 The Interior (Masqueray)

3.6 The Side Elevation (Masqueray)

Executive Building Committee meeting on that date, it was decided to distribute metal savings banks to the children of the Archdiocese, so that they too might set aside their resources for the new cathedral.[35] In the Spring of 1906 the banks were distributed,[36] and their proceeds over the next several years were supplemented by the silver dollars offered by candidates for confirmation in parishes under Ireland's jurisdiction.

Through the early stages of fund-raising, Ireland expressed satisfaction with the growing generosity of his people. He could justly have claimed some of the credit for it, given his active role in the fund-raising process. On August 1, 1905, copies of *The New Cathedral of St. Paul; Letter of the Most Reverend Archbishop* were distributed in every parish. Published simultaneously in German, French, Polish, and Bohemian, as well as English, the lengthy pamphlet was a master-stroke of public relations. Ireland emphasized that the building would be seen as the symbol of Catholic honor and vitality in the upper Northwest. Its people would no longer tolerate the absence of a structure grand enough to express their achievements and aspirations. He invited all to give. Those who contributed would feel a personal exhilaration upon the project's completion."...All will give as God permits them to give," concluded the Archbishop. "There should be no one who, entering the Cathedral, is not able to say — it is mine. I have put into the making of this great monument a stone that is mine. The stone, perchance, is small, but there it is; and, since it was the measure of my best will, God will reward it, as the earnest of my faith and love."[37] Ireland also delivered scores of addresses to both urban and rural congregations, always repeating the slogan, "A Great State, A Great City, A Great Cathedral," along with its challenge, "The New Cathedral now building is the grandest work ever undertaken for the greatness of the City of St. Paul. Will You Help Build It?"[38] Of all Ireland's speeches, the most profitable was delivered at a subscribers' picnic held on Independence Day, 1906, at the State Fairgrounds. Ireland's remarks were reinforced by those of Governor J.A. Johnson. Total receipts of the day amounted to $9,600, to add to the $524,200 in pledges already received.

By mid-1906, construction was about to begin. A site had been acquired, the final architectural plans had been approved, and subscriptions continued to pour into Smith's office in the Union Block. The meetings and discussions would now take second place to the sounds of shovels, hammers, and chisels.

3.8 The Cathedral of Saint Paul. The Interior

3.7 The Cathedral of Saint Paul. The Exterior.
"If [this] Cathedral were in Italy, thousands...would go there to see it as a classic piece of Renaissance 14th century architecture" (Cass Gilbert).

Chapter Four

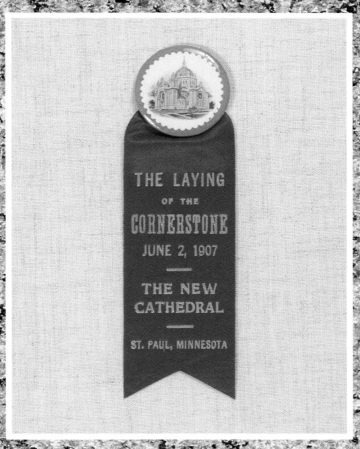

Growth: From Cornerstone to Dome, 1906-1914

Overleaf: A Souvenir of the Laying of the Cornerstone, June 2, 1907

eyond Archbishop Ireland's perorations and Masqueray's flawlessly executed design lay the daily realities of measurements, materials, labor, and finances. On January 18, 1906, the architect received the Executive Building Committee's approval of his specifications and working drawings for the crypt up to the level of the water table. Construction continued during the next eight years, interrupted only by the most severe winter weather, and despite repeated challenges and frustrations. By mid-1914, there were many who would see in the successful completion of the exterior fabric something only slightly less than miraculous. The work was executed with extraordinary determination, ability, faith, and through the collaboration of a handful of clerical and lay leaders.

Concerns over the Site

In early 1906, the Kittson property was found to be too small to accommodate the Cathedral and its monumental approaches as envisioned by Masqueray. While the land measured 233½ feet wide and 293½ deep, the plans called for a structure two hundred and seventy-four feet long and two hundred and fourteen feet wide.[1] The Executive Building Committee therefore sought to purchase the Berkey property which lay directly behind the building site. Negotiations broke down quickly since the owner wanted $80,000 for the land, and the Archdiocese was prepared to offer no more than $40,000. The Committee decided, on November 14, 1906, that continued bargaining was useless.[2] With expansion into the Dayton-Selby corridor blocked, Ireland and his associates turned to the south side of Summit Avenue, to the McNaught and Webber properties, listed by the City Planning Commission as Lots 10, 11, 12, 13, 14, and 15 of Fuller's Subdivision of Block 87, Dayton and Irvine's Addition. These parcels were acquired for $29,500. To link the two sites the Committee drew up a plan to move Summit Avenue ninety feet to the south, thus reducing its curvature (fig. 4.1). The Board of Public Works approved the proposal in early August, but with two conditions: that the Archdiocese would deed to the city a part of the McNaught-Webber lots to reroute Summit Avenue, and that it would pay for the transfer of water mains and new paving.[3] The Committee agreed.

During the negotiations over the course of Summit Avenue, Ireland contacted the Twin City Rapid Transit Company about its proposed tunnel under St. Anthony Hill. He was particularly concerned about the effect of streetcar vibrations within the tunnel which was projected to follow Selby Avenue adjacent to the Cathedral (fig. 4.2).

He was told that tunnel construction would begin the next winter, and that an ornamental iron "Cathedral Station" would be included.[4] Although the proposed station would go far to mitigate one criticism of the cathedral site, that nobody would climb steep St. Anthony Hill to attend Mass,[5] Archbishop Ireland was not reassured until engineers from the Chicago firm of Pierce, Neiler and Richardson concluded in January 1907, that the tunnel posed no threat to the Cathedral foundations.[6] But disappointment followed reassurance as the Transit Company soon abandoned the station plan as "impracticable and dangerous."[7]

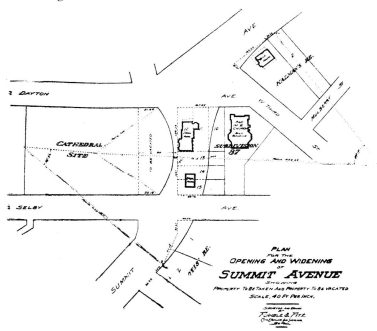

4.1 Plan for the Rerouting of Summit Avenue at the Site of the New Cathedral, 1906

Funds and Fabric: The First Steps

Masqueray presented his cost estimates at an Executive Building Committee meeting of July 5, 1906. Calling the figures "liberal" — he expected actual expenses to be lower — he estimated the cost of the structure as originally designed but without the dome, at $1,000,000. He expected the dome to add another $200,000 to the total. However, this projection was larger than even Ireland himself had anticipated. He responded that

> ...there were certain parts of the structure that could be well left to the future for completion, such as the chapels, ornamentations, etc. He thought...that by leaving unfinished certain portions, the edifice could be wholly completed exteriorly and interiorly fitted for occupancy and look very well for a total cost of one million dollars.[8]

4.2 Entrance to the Selby Avenue Tunnel

For the first time, it was clear that the Cathedral would become an ongoing enterprise, requiring the dedication of more than one generation to bring it to its final form.

On July 24, Masqueray completed full working plans for the first half of the foundation, including top grading and excavation. The Building Sub-committee solicited bids and seven firms entered the competition.[9] On August 16, the Committee awarded the contract to Lauer Brothers Construction Company of St. Paul, which had submitted the low bid of $72,750 ($4,823 for fifty-five days of grading, plus $67,927 for two hundred days of excavating and masonry work).[10] Between the signing of the contract on September 5 and the start of work in early November, Masqueray, aided by Chief Consulting Engineer Owen Brainard, commissioned a number of test borings on the site. The ground, a mixture of clean sand, gravel, and clay, was pronounced "capable of carrying the full loads imposed upon it so long as it is properly retained, settled and tamped before the laying of the concrete foundations."[11]

So satisfied was the Executive Building Committee with the Lauer Brothers' work, that on February 26, 1907, it gave them the contract for the second half of the foundation (figs. 4.3, 4.4). There was no competition, and

4.3 Setting the Foundation, 1906

their estimate of $94,960 was accepted.[12] The firm was not, however, to be responsible for the completion of the crypt interior. Masqueray had not yet finished the working plans for it. According to Ireland's long-range view of the previous July, the crypt interior would not be completed until several years later, and then by other firms.

4.4 Work on the Upper Foundation, 1907

By early 1907, the Committee confronted the issue of the stone to be used for the building's outside walls. The Committee agreed with Masqueray that the lower courses should be of granite, but this did not resolve the issue, since the architect had proposed several kinds of granite, each with important physical and aesthetic, as well as financial, advantages and liabilities. Though St. Cloud granite was plentiful, "there is no equipment at that place, which is equal to filling any large contract and furnishing the stone on time." Ortonville granite was too dark in color, and in any case, the quarry's owners showed no interest in so large an undertaking, preferring only to provide some columns for the interior. Indiana limestone, extracted at Bedford, was excellent, readily available, and, at $1.50 per cubic foot, the least costly of the materials proposed. Light-colored Vermont granite, at $2.50 per cubic foot, was more expensive, but cheaper to lay.[13] In the end, a special sub-committee chaired by Masqueray selected Rockville granite, quarried some ten miles from St. Cloud. Gray-pink in color, its high quartz content caused it to sparkle in the sunlight. The contract between the Archdiocese and Clark & McCormack, owners of the well-equipped quarry, was signed in May, to permit the extraction of $51,239 worth of granite, over a four-year period.[14]

The Laying of the Cornerstone

As the work continued, Ireland and the Committee decided that the laying of the cornerstone should be a very special ceremony, "a magnificent affair,...the occasion of as great a celebration as is possible to make it."[15] Since there had been no formal groundbreaking, the events of June 2, 1907, would be the first opportunity for the Archbishop and his people to celebrate not only the completion of the first stage of construction, but also the dedication and generosity of thousands of Minnesota Catholics. This ceremony would not be the last of its kind — others were already being planned to herald other stages of completion — but it remained the grandest and most memorable to be held over the eight-year period of construction.[16] The *St. Paul Pioneer Press,* which estimated the crowd at sixty thousand, would label the ceremony "the greatest church event in the history of the Northwest."[17]

Weather-wise the day was perfect: sunny and warm. By two o'clock in the afternoon, the area around the cathedral site overflowed with spectators from every part of the state. At half past two, an array of religious and civil dignitaries mounted the platform: four archbishops, thirty bishops, Senator Clapp, Governor Johnson, Mayor Smith, and other state and city officials. For the next ninety minutes some thirty thousand men, carrying the banners of the Knights of Columbus, the Ancient Order of Hibernians, and other Catholic societies, filed past the platform, in what was later hailed as the greatest parade in the city's history, with the possible exception of that of the G.A.R. in 1896. For drama, however, the spectacle of 1907 owned no superior; processing behind the College of St. Thomas cadets and representatives from every Archdiocesan parish and mission was the eighty-four-year-old Isaac Labissonniere, the sole survivor of the team which had built Galtier's log chapel.[18]

The copper box, sealed during the parade and placed in the cornerstone, measured six by twelve by fourteen inches, and contained items selected to illustrate the progress of the Church in Minnesota over the previous half-century. The box contained the following:

A copy of the *Jubilee History of the Diocese of St. Paul.*

Wiltzius' *Catholic Directory,* for the year 1907.

The *Directory of the City of St. Paul,* for 1907.

A copy of the addresses delivered on the occasion by Archbishop Ireland, Governor Johnson, Senator Clapp, Mayor Smith, and Judge William L. Kelly.

A complete set of the *Cathedral Bulletin.*

A photograph of the log chapel on Bench Street, built by Father Galtier in 1841.

A photograph of the same chapel with the addition made by Father Ravoux in 1847.

A photograph of the second cathedral built by Bishop Cretin on the corner of Sixth and Wabasha Streets, in 1851.

A photograph of the third cathedral built by Bishop Cretin in 1858.

Portraits of Galtier, Cretin, Ravoux, Grace, Ireland, and Father Anatole Oster.

The Saturday issue, June 1, 1907, of the *St. Paul Dispatch.*

The Sunday issue, June 2, 1907, of the *Minneapolis Tribune.*

The Sunday issue, June 2, 1907, of the *St. Paul Pioneer Press.*

The Saturday issue, June 1, 1907, of the *St. Paul Daily News.*

The Saturday issue, June 1, 1907, of the *Minneapolis Journal.*

The last issue of the *Northwestern Chronicle,* St. Paul.

The last issue of *Der Wanderer,* St. Paul.

The last issue of the *Irish Standard* of Minneapolis.

The register of the St. Paul Seminary, 1906-1907.

The catalogue of the College of St. Thomas, 1906-1907.

The catalogue of the College of St. Catherine, 1906-1907.

The catalogue of the Convent of the Visitation, 1906-1907.

The catalogue of St. Joseph's Academy, 1906-1907.

The catalogue of St. Agatha's Conservatory, 1906-1907.

The catalogue of Villa Maria, Frontenac, Minnesota.

The catalogue of Bethlehem Academy, Faribault, Minnesota.

The catalogue of Holy Angels Academy, Minneapolis.

Coins of United States issue, 1907.

Stamps of the Jamestown Exposition.

Lists of all committees.

A parchment written in Latin and setting forth the details of the ceremony, with the usual forms of such documents.[19]

Accompanied by an eighteen-voice seminary choir, Bishop James McGolrick of Duluth blessed the stone and placed it in position (fig. 4.5). He then proceeded to bless the foundations. Two of the stone's sides carried Latin inscriptions. On its Summit Avenue face was carved a statement of thanksgiving:

4.5 *The Laying of the Cornerstone, June 2, 1907*

1841-1907
Succeeding to the lowly chapel — built of old by the river's bank — from which our fair city received its glorious name, this noble temple rises; a solemn testimony to the growth of Holy Church, a generous offering of love and gratitude to the Almighty God, of all things Lord and Ruler.[20]

The Dayton Avenue face memorialized the events of the day, concluding with the motto of Pius X:

To God in Unity and Trinity. The sacred, auspicious stone of this metropolitan temple, bidden to bear the name of Saint Paul, was duly laid on the second day of June, A.D. 1907.

To restore all things in Christ.[21]

The addresses began following Ireland's reading of a cabled benediction from the Pope and a telegram of congratulations from President Roosevelt. Then, in a voice still full of its "old-time eloquence," he delivered what many considered to be his greatest speech.[22] Ireland recalled the growth of Northwestern Catholicism during the previous sixty-six years:

The solitary Galtier lives in seven bishops, in eight hundred priests. The few Catholics who formed his flock — from the Mississippi to the Missouri — are over the half million. The lowly chapel has multiplied itself into the thousand churches, around which cluster in the hundreds the prosperous homes of charity and learning.[23]

Thanking God for such progress, he pledged the new Cathedral as a sign of gratitude and faith in an age in which some in the name of science doubted the existence of God or denied the Divinity of Jesus. In a thankless and skeptical world the Cathedral on the hill would symbolize the Church's centuries-old mission of evangelizing all humanity, to create not only virtuous men and women, but also loyal citizens.

Following the Archbishop's remarks, Judge E. W. Bazille, chairman of the civic portion of the program and a member of the Executive Building Committee, spoke as did Mayor Smith, Governor Johnson, Senator Clapp, and Judge William L. Kelly, the Cathedral's unofficial poet laureate. The ceremony ended with the firing of a salute by Battery A, First Artillery, Minnesota National Guard, after which all joined in the intonation of the *Te Deum.*

Unfair Criticism, Real Problems

The elation resulting from the cornerstone ceremony was well-timed, for it cushioned Ireland and the Executive Building Committee against a number of oftentimes ridiculous allegations over the next several months. Ireland was no stranger to controversy, but he was irritated by a continuous series of rumors which had dogged construction from the start, and which by mid-1907 seemed to be growing. As early as May 1904, Ireland denied newspaper reports both in the Twin Cities and Chicago that the Cathedral would cost millions of dollars: "[The] figures...are extravagantly high. All stories of great gifts to the...building fund are purely imaginary."[24] Four years later, the rumor resurfaced. Charles H. F. Smith informed Ireland, who was in Rome at the time, that the cost of the building was to be $4,500,000, and that it would require twelve years to complete.[25]

> What you write... [responded Ireland]...is amusing and somewhat annoying. Really, our American press surpasses all bounds in its sensationalism. Here in Rome, for instance, correspondents of certain American papers unblushingly admit that they forge items of news, that their papers demand that something be sent forward, and so, something is sent, true or false.[26]

Nevertheless, by 1907, subscriptions and gifts were showing unmistakable signs of slowing down. On June 25, the Archbishop appointed a committee of laymen to solicit donations from non-Catholics, but the initiative was inexplicably still-born. As income failed to parallel mounting costs, Ireland, in January 1908, levied an "assessment" on each parish, the specific amount to be determined by the financial state of each congregation. He hoped to obtain an additional one million dollars.[27] At the same time, Father John J. Lawler (fig. 4.6), a member of the Executive Building Committee, was commissioned to solicit funds from prominent Catholics who had not as

of yet donated.[28] Polite reminders were also sent to those subscribers in arrears.

Work on the Superstructure

In the midst of rumors and financial problems, and as work on the crypt continued, Masqueray completed the exterior elevation drawings. In early 1909, he also finished the main floor plan and granite details. In July, two competitions were held, the first to provide material for the superstructure, and the second to construct it up to the cornice line of the dome and the intersection of the walls with the roof. Eight firms bid on the material: three proposed granite; three, limestone; the seventh, marble; and the eighth, both marble and limestone.[29] Deciding on limestone, the Committee chose a Wisconsin company, which then immediately raised its estimate $15,000. On

4.6 Father (later Bishop) John J. Lawler

September 17, the Committee terminated the agreement, and awarded a new contract to Clark & McCormack, who had submitted the lowest bid among companies proposing to use granite. To justify the shift in materials and the greater expense (Rockville granite cost twice as much as Bedford limestone), the members of the Committee pointed out that granite was more permanent *and* a Minnesota product.[30]

There were no complications in the selection of a construction company. P. M. Hennessy bested Lauer Brothers with an estimate more than $20,000 lower than that presented by the firm which had so rapidly laid the Cathedral's foundations. The contract was signed on August 9, 1909, and work began on the walls during the spring of 1910. As the building inched upward to claim an ever more prominent place on the skyline, excitement among Catholics also grew. Post- 1910 accounts of the Executive Building Committee meetings are imbued with feelings of anticipation and renewed energy. No matter that the deliveries of granite were sometimes late; no matter that some of the blocks arrived defective.[31] With optimism and momentum, Ireland and his colleagues calmly and successfully solved these problems by mid-1910.

In Search of Publicity

A sense of expectation, however, is best enjoyed when it is shared, and as the piers and walls rose, the Archbishop took several initiatives designed to intensify interest during the final phase of construction. Brilliant examples of public relations, they were prefaced by Ireland's announcement of 1909, amid much fanfare, that the Pope had blessed all subscribers to the Cathedral fund. On September 20, 1910, he hosted a second ceremony to place the lintel on the southwest door of the transept. Vincenzo Cardinal Vannutelli, Papal legate to the recent International Eucharistic Congress at Montreal, presided. As he toured the different parts of the structure, arm-in-arm with Ireland, Vannutelli "made exclamations of pleasure in Italian...and waved his hand enthusiastically," delighting the hundreds of onlookers.[32]

To assure both solicitors and donors that their sacrifices had not been in vain, the Executive Building Committee purchased three hundred copies of the July 13th issue of *American Architect,* for distribution to all pastors. The periodical referred to the growing edifice as one of the great religious monuments in America.[33] And in January 1911, the Committee sponsored an illustrated lecture by J. Howard Albert on "the great cathedrals of the world, with special reference to the Cathedral of Saint Paul." Albert, touted as "a world-wide traveler...[who]...speaks from personal observation of the views he exhibits," was followed at the lectern by Ireland, Governor Eberhart, Mayor Keller, Senator Coller, and other officials.[34]

Completion of the Roof and Dome

Less than two years after the placement of the "Vannutelli lintel," on July 18, 1912, the granite cross was hoisted to the top of the one-hundred-and-fifteen-foot- high facade (fig. 4.7). In a simple ceremony, Ireland blessed the cross,

which weighed 5½ tons and measured 10′6″ by 5′2″, and delivered a brief address. As he had done previously, Ireland praised the site, Masqueray's design, the generosity of Minnesota's Catholics, the quality of the materials used, and the excellent workmanship. More importantly, he looked to the next ceremony, "that of putting into place the cross on the top of the cupola — the signal that the whole exterior is completed. When will that day come? I wish I could name it. May we hope it will be somewhere in the midsummer of 1913."[35]

4.7 Erection of the Granite Cross on the Facade, July 18, 1912

On September 9, 1912, the W. J. Hoy Company won the contract for the roof and dome, which included steel framing and the setting of all granite above the cornice line. Hoy's estimate had been lower than those of its four competitors, two of whom — Lauer Brothers and P. M. Hennessy — had already enjoyed a working relationship with the Executive Building Committee.[36] Yet the Committee soon found that even Hoy's low price of $98,473 was more than it could finance at that time. The dome, Ireland concluded, would remain uncompleted until some later date. But several prominent St. Paul businessmen stepped in to solve the problem. On September 19, they gathered at a luncheon in the St. Paul Hotel, to find some way of raising the required $100,000. During discussion of various fund-raising schemes, Otto Bremer rose to suggest that he and his colleagues pledge an amount equal to what they already had given. The sum was reached before the end of the meal, and presented to the Archdiocese, as the "Archbishop Ireland Testimonial Fund," in January 1913.[37]

So quickly was the work on the dome carried out that

4.8 The Superstructure under Construction

4.9 The Dome under Construction, 1912

4.10 The Framing of the Lantern on the Dome, 1912

on December 1 the last stone was set on one of its eight turrets (figs. 4.8, 4.9, 4.10). The accompanying celebration was poorly attended and brief, due to the harsh weather, but Ireland's enthusiasm and eloquence remained unaffected by the severe cold. He pointed to the Cathedral's symbolism as the home of the Eucharistic God and the refuge of a beleaguered humanity.[38]

The exterior was declared officially completed on May 18, 1914, when, in the presence of a large crowd, a steel cross, fourteen-by-eight feet, was blessed and then hoisted 306½ feet to the top of the dome, where it was secured by steel supports anchored in the metal plates surrounding the lantern.[39] But this triumphal scene carried a note of tragedy. Earlier that spring, a wind-blown beam had struck a steelworker. He fell to the concrete floor and was killed instantly.[40]

spent nearly four years perched high atop the maze of scaffolding obscuring the front of the edifice. There, using only mallets and chisels, they transformed the large, rough masses of stone implanted during the construction (fig. 4.11). (A forge was set up near the site to repair and sharpen the frequently broken tools.) The rigorous effort was worthwhile, for the effect of the Michelangelesque composition was — and indeed remains — scintillating. "If you stand on the terrace before the main portals, you cannot help but be impressed by the rugged splendor of the richly carved facade....The sculptures were conceived and have been executed in a style entirely harmonious with the heroic proportions of the structure."[42] Yet their aesthetic impact is not their sole, or even primary, *raison d'être*. Their strong decorative appeal is secondary to their symbolism as expressions of a system of belief. They

4.11 The Facade with Uncarved Tympanum, 1912

The Facade Sculpture: A Lesson in Stone
Highlighting the completed exterior was the pedimental sculpture of the main facade, the work of Leon Hermant (1866-1936) of Chicago. Given the commission by the Executive Building Committee in October 1910,[41] the sculptor and his team of carvers, headed by John Garratti,

remind onlookers in a dramatic way that the Cathedral of St. Paul, like its ancestors in medieval Europe, is not only a house of worship, but a great theology book in stone. The lesson which bursts forth from its facade is unmistakably John Ireland's.[43]

Chiseled within the pediment immediately beneath

4.13 Faith and Science. Detail from the Sculpture of the Facade

4.12 Christ and the Apostles Flanked by Saints Peter and Paul. Detail from the Sculpture of the Facade

the granite cross is a sixty-foot-wide rendition of Christ and the twelve apostles, under which is carved in Latin the great commission from Matthew 28:19, "Go therefore and teach ye all nations" (fig. 4.12). Flanking the inscription on either side of the monumental arch, are low-relief figures of Saints Peter and Paul, each twelve feet in height, symbolizing the human leadership through which the Divine commission was passed down and carried out. In the center of the archway, between the rose window and the main portal, sit two large and uneasily posed allegorical figures, carved by Oscar Anderson (fig. 4.13). Together, they measure twenty-seven by eight feet. One, representing faith, brandishes a cross. The other, representing science, carries a torch. In themselves these symbols have little meaning, but as an integral part of the facade, viewed from the pediment down to the portal, they express the conviction that Christ's challenge to His followers, while guided by His Church, is realized in the collaboration of true religion and true science. "Church and age! They pulsate alike: the God of nature works in one, the God of supernatural revelation in the other....Unite them in the name of humanity, in the name of God": this is the Irelandian plea in stone. Placed between the figures is a garlanded cartouche bearing, in Latin, the words of John 1:9, "He was the true light that enlightens every man that comes into this world" — a reference to the conviction that all truth comes from the God-man in Whose honor the Cathedral was built.

The completed exterior was a moving indication that the edifice on the already popularly renamed "Cathedral Hill" was designed for learning as much as prayer. When work on the interior began, in April 1914, this dual purpose would be further underscored.

Chapter Five

Refinement: Work on the Interior, 1914-1918

Overleaf: *The Chapel of St. Peter.* St. Peter

Interestingly, the Petrine pose is reputedly of Johannine inspiration, meaning that this statue's posture supposedly reproduces Archbishop Ireland's oratorical stance.

With the completion of the exterior, a frantic effort was launched in late 1914 to equip the interior, if only minimally, for liturgical use. The Archbishop had decided that the first Mass was to be held on Easter Sunday, 1915, prodding the architectural team by his daily visits to the building, during which he would inspect every newly added detail and every newly opened perspective.[1]

Earlier in the year it had been agreed that the ceiling and dome had to be completed before the structure was opened to the public. Accordingly, in March 1914, a competition for the work was announced, and four companies presented bids.[2] On April 3, the Executive Building Committee selected the firm of Beil & Hermant of Chicago and New York. Its estimate of $51,867 was not the lowest — in fact, it exceeded the lowest quote by almost $11,000 — but "it seemed to be the sentiment of the [Committee members] that with Beil & Hermant,...they could be sure of a thoroughly artistic and satisfactory ceiling, while with the other bidders it was not so certain....The work should be assigned to an artist, and not merely [to] one who was skilled in plain plastering."[3] The application of the ornamental plaster, however, was a much less straightforward affair. Ireland's prodding notwithstanding, the work went very slowly, almost stopping by December, as many of the most skilled and efficient craftsmen returned to their native France for military service.[4] To compensate for the loss of time and to meet the Archbishop's deadline, American crews worked around the clock through January 1915. Perhaps the most fitting tribute to their dedication and stamina is the fact that the first Mass in the new Cathedral was held one week earlier than Ireland's projected date.

A Farewell to the Old Cathedral

As plans were being drawn, in 1914, for a dedication ritual comparable in grandeur to the cornerstone-laying ceremony seven years earlier, they also were being made for an appropriately solemn farewell to the old Cathedral. The fifty-six-year-old edifice, so integral a part of Minnesota Catholic history, was set to be demolished in the autumn, to make way for an office building. Because of its importance to so many people, Ireland decided that two days would be set aside for the valediction.[5] On Sunday, August 30, 1914, Bishop Thomas O'Gorman of Sioux Falls celebrated a Pontifical Mass (fig. 5.1). The selection of O'Gorman was apt, for he and Ireland had been the first two seminarians of the Diocese of St. Paul. Included within the overflowing congregation were several pioneers, Cath-

olic and non-Catholic alike, who had witnessed Cretin's laying of the cornerstone in 1856. In his sometimes emotional sermon, Ireland urged his listeners to recall the half-century of sights and sounds which had passed among those austere walls:

...Look well around: for the last time see what so long you have loved to see: call back in memory the years gone by, all that those years do mean to you. Here knelt your fathers and mothers, your sons, daughters and friends — hence they were

5.1 The Final Mass in the Third Cathedral of Saint Paul, August 30, 1914

borne to the cemetery. Here you were baptized, received your first communion, were married. Here, so often, you heard mass and prayed. Here, you listened to the word of God preached from the pulpit. Here, you sought in the Sacrament of Penance the remission of your sins, in the Sacrament of the Eucharist the food of divine life. Here, you prayed and heard the voice of God bidding you be of good cheer amid trials and suffering, bidding you be strong against temptation and sin: here, so often, in anticipation you tasted the joys of Heaven, and in the depth of your souls sensibly felt the blessed hope of immortality in the bosom of the Almighty God. Truly the Cathedral has been for you 'the house of God, the gate of Heaven.' Could you but have loved it? Could you but be thrilled with emotion as your lips open to say, farewell?[6]

This evocation reaffirmed Ireland's conviction that a cathedral was a compilation of personal faith and individual memories as much as it was a skillful combination of marble, stone, wood, and glass. As such, it continued to live, even after demolition, revivifying itself in ever more impressive forms:

But hearken — what says the old Cathedral? Resurgam — I will arise. I do not die: the third Cathedral of St. Paul, no more than the second, or the first, does not die. Into newer life, into fresher and more resplendent beauty I will arise, this time unchanged and unchangeable adown the centuries.[7]

It was on this optimistic, triumphal note that the third Cathedral of St. Paul was relinquished by its Ordinary.

The Opening of the New Cathedral

The first liturgy in the new Cathedral was held on Palm Sunday, March 28, 1915. After worshipping for seven months at the new Cathedral school, parishioners eagerly joined their co-religionists from throughout the Twin Cities area at a six a.m. Mass celebrated by the Archbishop. The interior was painfully bare: while the flooring and Oklahoma red-oak pews had been installed, the walls were of whitewashed brick, all the chapels were empty, and none of the stained glass had been installed. For a time, the altar, episcopal chair, and pipe organ from the old Cathedral would be used, while in the south tower the old Cathedral's bell would continue to call the faithful as it had for over a half-century. But if the trappings of that early-hour celebration were spartan, the experience turned out to be rich. The vast structure was completely filled with worshipers, disproving critics who claimed that it would never be filled. During the Mass, as Ireland turned to the congregation for the first time, he was so overcome that he broke down and sobbed, "a most unusual thing for this soldier-spirited man."[8] Some twenty-five hundred received Holy Communion that morning, first among them being the Archbishop's own sister, Mother Seraphine, Provincial of the Sisters of St. Joseph. Two more equally crowded Masses were held at the new Cathedral that Sunday. At eight o'clock three thousand members of the Ancient Order of Hibernians and of their Ladies Auxiliary attended Father Lawrence Ryan's Mass, the first of hundreds to be offered in the structure for civic groups and charitable organizations. At ten o'clock, Bishop Lawler celebrated a Solemn Pontifical Mass. In his sermon Ireland pointed to the unfinished stones as "our supreme act of faith, our solemn, near-silent Credo."[9] The day's festivities ended with evening Benediction.

The well-attended liturgies of Holy Week did not mitigate any of the "unusual joy" born of Palm Sunday's three Masses; the spirit of Easter brought it to a peak.[10] On Low Sunday, April 11, Ireland formally dedicated the building. After blessing both the exterior and interior, he presided at a Solemn Pontifical Mass celebrated by Bishop McGolrick of Duluth. Bishop O'Gorman addressed a congregation of more than four thousand, including a dozen prelates. He chose for his theme, "Know you not, that you are the temple of God, and that the Spirit of God dwelleth in you?" (1 Corinthians 3:16).[11] After the sermon, the Bishop read three letters congratulating Ireland and his people on their achievement. Written in his own hand, Pope Benedict XV's remarks expressed delight upon hearing that "this Cathedral has grown into a temple of such amplitude and such magnificence and such elegance of form as truly to merit to be called monumental."[12] Pietro Cardinal Gasparri, Vatican Secretary of State, and Diomede Cardinal Falconio, former Apostolic Delegate to the United States, deemed the new Cathedral the crowning accomplishment of an estimable episcopal career.[13]

Ireland's greatest glory it may have been, but one not without critics who expressed concern about the structure's poor acoustics and distracting immensity. Father Ryan, soon to be appointed Cathedral rector, later described the background and antidote to these negative assessments:

This was, of course, the largest church in the city. People were accustomed to small churches, and hence much of the criticism about acoustics and about difficulty to pray and hear Mass devoutly in such a large place, was unfair. Soon all of this disappeared. The great majority had, of course, never seen the grand Cathedrals of the old world, and the characteristic impressiveness of Cathedral lines, 'majestic and heavenly,' had not dawned upon them. Four or five years passed before this idea took hold of the popular imagination.[14]

No doubt, too, working on the popular imagination was the greater refinement of the interior, which dispelled the anxiety of trying to worship in what seemed to some a cavernous warehouse.

The Chapels of St. Peter and St. Joseph

As the Cathedral passed into regular daily use, Masqueray designed the chapels of St. Peter and St. Joseph. Built with funds donated by Mrs. James McCahill of Lake City, in memory of her late husband, the shrine to the first Pope was begun in December 1916, completed in May 1917, and dedicated on June 30, 1920 (fig. 5.2).[15] Work within the forty-one-by-twenty-six- by-twenty-two-foot area was done by Italian craftsmen, a fitting choice since most of the facing came from the famous quarries at Carrara. The walls and columns were of Sienna Gold, the altar, of Sienna Gray, and the semi- circular credence tables flank-

Latin the words by which Christ bestowed upon Peter the leadership of His people: "You are Peter and upon this rock I will build my Church" (Matthew 16:18). The words were a perfect complement to the majestic rendition of the saint, which, according to its creator, was designed to exalt the power of the Papacy. Other inscriptions, also in Latin, were set in ornamental niches within the side walls.

5.2 The Chapel of St. Peter, 1916-1917

ing the altar, of brown marble. Only the panel behind the tabernacle, guarded by a solid bronze door and surmounted by Hermant's seven-foot-high statue of St. Peter in white marble, was not of Italian origin; it was French Broccatello. The white marble floor was interspersed with variously colored strips of *Giallo Fantastico* imported from Serravezza, Italy; in its center was laid a large circular design containing the traditional cross and halo, each featuring a combination of all the marbles used in the chapel. Within the apse, which replicated on a smaller scale the general lines of the Cathedral, were inscribed in

Carved on the Gospel side was the dedication "to the Almighty God, under the title of St. Peter, Prince of the Apostles"; on the Epistle side was placed a request to "pray for the soul of James McCahill, beloved spouse, who was born in 1853 and died in 1911." The stuccoed ceiling was, like the statue, the work of Hermant; it depicted the three great events in St. Peter's life — his calling by Christ, commission as head of the Church, and martyrdom — all done in low relief and colored in the same tints as the marble below (fig. 5.3). Altogether the decoration of the chapel cost some $30,000. Public reaction was mixed.

5.3 The Chapel of St. Peter. Detail of the Ceiling

According to Father Ryan, "...the work was...much to the delight of those who knew what gold terra marble is; much to the disgust of not a few who thought that all marble is white!"[16]

The unimpeded progress of the work in the chapel of St. Peter was, unfortunately, not repeated in the furnishing of the slightly larger (forty-one-by-thirty-six-by-twenty-two- foot) memorial to the foster father of Jesus. Scheduled for completion in December 1917, the chapel of St. Joseph was finished in May of the following year, due to the war (fig. 5.4). A rich mélange of marble was provided by the E. M. Lohmann Company of St. Paul: Breccia Violetta, a golden-yellow Italian variety with dark veining, for the columns; American Danbury Cream, a product of Vermont, for the walls, altar, and floor border; Tennessee Pink, for the remainder of the floor; and German rose and black Formosa, for the panel behind Hermant's statue of the patron.[17] Three Latin inscriptions were set into the marble. Ribboning the apse was an exhortation: "Let us praise our God in honor of Blessed Joseph our Protector." The wall on the Epistle side bore the dedicatory statement, "To the Almighty God, under the title of Saint Joseph, Patron of the Universal Church as well as our own personal guardian and helper." Directly opposite, on the Gospel side, was incised the recognition of the donors: "This chapel, the gift of the Sisters of St. Joseph, their pupils and their friends." Acknowledgement of individual contributors was made by placing their names in a parchment volume, deposited within the altar. The ensemble was dedicated on July 20, 1920.

The Death of Masqueray

Shortly after completing the chapel designs, Masqueray turned to the sanctuary. That his original intention was to create a large main altar surmounted by a baldachin, is clear from his earliest sketches of the interior. By 1917 a model of the baldachin was built. Somewhat heavier than the one eventually installed a few years later, it was to be of masonry, supported by four spiral columns, and capped by finials.[18] If the model was stillborn, it was not because of any inherent defects in concept or design; it was, rather, because of Masqueray's death on May 26, 1917 (fig. 5.5).

The architect had been in poor health since the previous Christmas, but no one, including his doctors, had expected him to die.[19] While riding the streetcar to work, he was stricken with a uremic attack, lapsed into a coma, and only briefly regained consciousness. Ireland's office was flooded with condolences and tributes. All shared the sentiment of Archbishop Keane, who saw in Masqueray "the [true]...Christian gentleman...[whose] name will live enshrined in a great Cathedral, his creation."[20] At the funeral Mass Archbishop Ireland chose to dwell not on his friend's well- known piety, but on his cultured demeanor, charm, courtliness, and charity.[21] Though Ireland's rather stoic eulogy may not have shown it, his sense of loss must have been great, for

...[his] right hand was gone. How many hours the two dreamed and planned. Now they talked calmly, now they soared on the wings of enthusiasm, and Masqueray, throwing aside the halting English, broke into French until he had the Archbishop equally fluent and eloquent in [it]. Hands were going like a Dutch windmill.[22]

The Passing of the Archbishop

Less than a year and a half later, Ireland followed the architect in death. His health had steadily deteriorated through late 1917 and early 1918. As his illness grew worse, so did much of his enthusiasm for the building he had come to call the "dream of his mature years."[23] His last visit to the Cathedral was in the early winter of 1917-1918. Confined to a wheelchair, he had come to inspect the placement of the marble in the chapel of St. Joseph. After a brief look, he turned away. As he was taken out, he could barely lift his head to look into that dome which at one point in 1912 he feared would never be completed in his lifetime. During his final weeks he spent his time sitting on the porch of the Wilder House, located opposite the Cathedral and recently purchased to serve as the archiepiscopal residence. From that vantage point he would gaze on the structure for hours. He died on September 25, 1918. Over four thousand faithful joined twenty prelates and more than eight hundred priests at the funeral Mass celebrated by Bishop O'Gorman on October 2 (fig. 5.6). Even in death, however, Ireland influenced the future of the Cathedral. He was buried not in the crypt, but in Calvary Cemetery, "in the sunshine, out among my people."[24] Having set the precedent, the Archbishop of St.

5.4 The Chapel of St. Joseph, 1916-1918

5.5 Masqueray's Grave Marker, Calvary Cemetery, St. Paul
In the medallion above the architect's portrait stands a rendition of his masterpiece.

Paul assured that the crypt of his metropolitan church would remain a crypt in name only.

In a short period of time the new Cathedral of St. Paul had lost both its godparents. There were many, like Father Ryan, who lamented that they would not enjoy the realization of their dreams and dedication: Masqueray saw nothing of the completed interior, while Ireland was too ill to appreciate the little he was able to see. Moreover, there was a great deal of concern about the future of the work on the interior. Would the new Ordinary share the energetic Ireland's commitment to the project? Would the new architect possess Masqueray's sense of proportion and line? Such concerns, however, were short-lived. By the time of their passing, the Archbishop and the architect had succeeded in placing an indelible imprint on the edifice, so that after 1918 all work would continue to be guided by their theological and architectural visions. Excursions beyond these visions would only raise anger against the innovator.[25] And if the imprint was ineffaceable, so also was it distinguished. Visitors to the Cathedral, overwhelmed by its vastness, may forget that its pedigree is impeccable. It remains, seven decades after its dedication, the offspring of American Catholicism's highest ideals and one of European architecture's most inspired expressions.

5.6 The Funeral of Archbishop Ireland, October 2, 1918

Chapter Six

Maturity: The First Ryan Era, 1916-1940

Overleaf: St. Paul. *Detail from the Baldachin*

On March 25, 1919, Austin Dowling, former Bishop of Des Moines, was installed as the second Archbishop of St. Paul (fig. 6.1). From the very beginning, and throughout his eleven-year tenure, the shadow of his predecessor loomed large while the inevitable comparisons of the two prelates always redounded to the disadvantage of the fragile, reserved, and bookish successor. It is indeed ironic that this most likeable of men found difficulty in being accepted by his nostalgic clergy and laity. More to the point, it is sad that the major obstacle to that acceptance was nothing more than the simple fact that he was *not* John Ireland.[1]

Archbishop Austin Dowling

Adding to the poignancy of Dowling's situation was that the unfavorable comparisons obscured the new Archbishop's own strength of character and impressive abilities. Like Ireland, he was determined to make the faith relevant to the age. Though his strategy may have differed from that of his flamboyant predecessor — he preferred building Catholic minds to building monumental churches — his campaign was no less zealous. At the same time, he himself displayed that intellectual refinement which he hoped to instill in his community. To every question of belief and ecclesiastical procedure, he brought a subtle understanding of theology and a broad appreciation of the Church's history. It was, however, his reserved personality and reordering of archdiocesan priorities which led many during the days following his

installation to fear that the completion of the Cathedral might be delayed, or, worse, indefinitely postponed. Sensing the uneasiness, Dowling immediately promised that the work would be continued; more than that, the completion of the interior was listed among his most important goals.

What the Archbishop's relieved listeners could not have known, of course, was how well their leader, apparently the antithesis of the man-of-action, would fulfill his promise. Their doubts were soon dispelled by the additions to the interior. While the work followed the rapid pace of the "Roaring Twenties," it maintained a uniformly high artistic standard. Dowling brought his own highly developed aesthetic sense to the project, offering suggestions at every turn. Only the most harmonious and appropriate designs would be realized in his cathedral, and no detail, however small, was executed without first passing his scrutiny. Just as the exterior was the result of John Ireland's vision, the interior was the fruit of Austin Dowling's flawless artistic instinct, which suffused the daunting space of nave, transepts, and dome with warmth and serenity.

Monsignor Lawrence F. Ryan

But if the Archbishop guaranteed the quality of the work, it was the rector of the Cathedral, Monsignor Lawrence F.

6.2 *Monsignor Lawrence F. Ryan*

6.1 *Archbishop Austin Dowling*

Ryan (fig. 6.2), who kept it going on a day-to-day basis. Ryan had been named to his position by Archbishop Ireland in 1916, the "year of the three rectors."[2] Over the next quarter-of- a-century he brought the interior to a state of near- completion, while also constructing a sacristy and rectory. His success was the result of his incredible energy and unrelenting optimism. By all estimates he was an indefatigable clergyman, whose enthusiasm for the Cathedral was rivaled only by his love of people and dedication to truth. Before becoming rector, Ryan had worked among juvenile delinquents and the poor in St. Paul. In June 1916 he had volunteered as chaplain for the First Field Artillery of the Minnesota National Guard; only his appointment to the rectorate had prevented him from accompanying the unit to the scene of hostilities along the Mexican-American border.[3] His new commission, however, held challenges akin to those found in the military. Ireland's statement of appointment was carefully phrased: "You have all the rights and duties of a pastor. And your special work will be to finish the interior of the Cathedral."[4] He took this charge, which was renewed by Dowling, very seriously, executing it with a sometimes martial spirit worthy of his former comrades at Fort Snelling. To this drive he added an artistic sensitivity and profound spirituality on a par with those of his Archbishop. Often his leadership would be tried. In 1920, for example, at Dowling's request, he ended the Cathedral Building Fund, placing the principal financial responsibility for completion of the interior upon the people of the Cathedral parish.[5] In the end, he found the funds, and the work continued uninterrupted. If, in speaking of the edifice, he betrayed a "pride of proprietorship," it was certainly justified. Given the length of his association and his selfless efforts toward its completion, he had every right to call it "my Cathedral."

The Chapel of the Blessed Virgin Mary

Much of the earliest interior work done under Ryan had actually been conceived, if not also designed, under the aegis of his two predecessors. Such was the case with the chapel of the Blessed Virgin, the color scheme and decoration of which had been worked out by Masqueray in 1915.[6] Begun in February 1914, a campaign to collect donations from every Catholic woman in the Archdiocese was so successful that the contract for the marble was awarded by early 1917, and the chapel completed in April 1919. It was dedicated on May 28, 1921 (fig. 6.3).

As with the previously completed chapels of St. Peter and St. Joseph, the shrine to Mary featured a mixture of marbles within its forty-one-by-thirty-six-by-twenty-two-foot area: a blend of blue-white from the Carrara region, for the main walls; Italian Coralla, for the columns; and South American *Vert Claire,* for the panel behind Hermant's statue of the Blessed Virgin and Child. Modeled closely after the seventeenth-century statue of Mary and Jesus in the Church of Notre-Dame-des-Victoires, Paris, a copy of which Bishop Cretin brought with him to St. Paul in 1851 (see p. 9), this rendition was carved in Chicago, after which the final details were added by Hermant himself in St. Paul. Upon its completion, the sculptor adjudged it his masterpiece. Inscribed in Latin across the apse is the Archangel Gabriel's salutation: "Hail Mary, full of grace, the Lord is with you. Blessed are you among women" (Luke 1:28). Although an inscription recognizing the donors was planned for one of the side walls, it was never placed. However, within the altar, a parchment volume listing the names and donations of individual contributors was deposited.[7] Upon its dedication the chapel was provided with wooden kneelers, purchased at a cost of $500 by Mrs. John B. Meagher, wife of the Secretary of the Executive Building Committee.

Whitney Warren and the Baldachin

With the completion of the Marian chapel, Masqueray's designs were exhausted. Under Dowling and Ryan all remaining work on the interior would be done by a number of talented designers prepared to follow the artistic lead of the Frenchman. The first of these, Whitney Warren (1864-1943), was appointed by Ireland in late 1917, to produce an appropriate main altar and baldachin. Like Masqueray, with whom he had worked in New York, Warren was a graduate of the Ecole des Beaux-Arts, and was enjoying a growing reputation, due mainly to his designs for several Manhattan landmarks, including Grand Central Station and a number of prestigious hotels. Although he had no experience in ecclesiastical architecture, he was chosen because Mrs. George Theron Slade, née Charlotte Hill, the altar's donor, wanted a fellow New Yorker to receive the commission. Warren relished the opportunity to create the liturgical ensemble as a tribute to his former associate.[8]

By April 1918 Warren had produced three or four designs. At the end of August they were presented to the dying Archbishop Ireland who opted for the simplest: a colonnade of six twisting columns surmounted by a bronze crown. Yet the ease with which the design was selected, was not to be repeated through the construction process. Pressure from several quarters forced Warren to change a number of details on the original design; most notably, the columns so reminiscent of those supporting the canopy of St. Peter's in Rome. In the re-design, these were straightened, probably at the behest of Mrs. Slade.[9] Even after the contracts were signed and building begun, the project proceeded very slowly. Almost two years passed between the arrival of the first shipment of Italian marble in September 1922, and the completion of the gilding on the baldachin, in August 1924. Eschewing for once the patience for which he had become famous,

6.3 The Chapel of the Blessed Virgin Mary, 1914-1919

Dowling celebrated the first Mass within the still heavily scaffolded setting on May 22, 1924.

Once the scaffolding was removed, and the piece displayed in its entirety, frustration over repeated delays vanished in universal approbation. No better centerpiece could be imagined for Masqueray's cathedral: simple and grand, it harmonized effortlessly with its surroundings. In color as well as design it joined with the other architectural features of the interior, to create an overall effect, reinforcing the beauty and power of the neighboring pieces in the sanctuary. Considering its preponderant size and rich ornamentation, this was no meager achievement.

6.4 The Main Altar with Its Pre-1940 Setting

The altar itself was cut from light Botticino marble (fig. 6.4). Appended to its front was a panel of Spanish *Rojo Alicante* marble, bordered at the top by two varieties of Italian marble, Verona Red and the extremely rare *Giallo Fantastico*. Fixed to its rear was the dedicatory panel, with the following inscription in Latin:

In memory of a beloved father, James Jerome Hill, whose goodness was displayed prudently and philanthropically, Charlotte Hill Slade, a most dutiful daughter, lovingly donates this high altar of the temple cathedral recently erected by Archbishop John Ireland, on which the names of her natural parent and of her father in Christ are conjoined. 1923.

Around the altar were positioned six monolithic (i.e., single-piece) columns of black and gold Portora marble, each twenty-four feet in height and almost eight tons in weight (fig. 6.5). Capping these six black-robed guardians of the altar were cast bronze Corinthian capitals, which were crowned by a segmented ring of Verona Red. From this ring rose the bronze latticework canopy, decorated by Smiraldi of New York. Ensconced within the upper reaches of the canopy were three statues by Hermant. In an act of Divine adoration, two angels place wreaths on the bronze clouds above the tabernacle; the face of the one on the Epistle side was modeled after that of Dante Gabriel Rossetti's *Blessed Damozel* of 1871-1879.[10] Between them, and directly facing the nave, was placed St. Paul, the Apostle to the Gentiles (see p. 49). His right hand is raised in gesture, while his left holds the sword. At the crest of the entire fifty-seven-foot-high composition was implanted a cross, and immediately

6.5 The Baldachin

under it the shield, symbol of the Holy Spirit. Conceived and executed by anyone other than the gifted Warren, this combination of diverse symbols rendered in diverse materials might have proven too heavy and too busy — in short, disastrously overpowering. Happily, Warren's first foray into ecclesiastical design tempered massiveness with grace, solemnity with color, grandeur with lightness, and ornamentation with classical artistic restraint. In terms of sheer effect, it remains "one of the most successful decorations in American church architecture" (fig. 6.6).[11]

In 1926 Georgiana Slade added to her mother's magnificent gift by presenting Father Ryan with a crucifix

6.6 The Sanctuary Seen from the Base of the Dome

and six large candlesticks for use on the main altar. A product of seventeenth-century Flanders, the entire set was of hammered silver. Before its debut at the Holy Thursday Mass of 1926, it was gilded, to blend with its surroundings. At the same time, the original corpus on the crucifix, deemed inappropriate by the artistically hypersensitive rector, was replaced with one of ivory, donated to the Cathedral by Masqueray. All seven pieces remained on the altar until 1940, when they were replaced during the installation of the marble gradine ordered by Archbishop Murray.

In mid-1919 Dowling announced his decision to finish the southern half of the crypt for use as a sacristy, meeting room, and chapel. Fred Slifer and Frank Abrahamson, both of whom had trained under Masqueray, were commissioned to do the work, which consisted mainly of plastering. Begun in September 1919, the project was plagued from the first by labor unrest and rapidly rising prices. The area was not completed until April 1920, five months behind schedule, and with a cost overrun of $23,000.[12]

Rectory and Sacristy

Of all Masqueray's successors, however, none left a greater stamp on the Cathedral than Charles D. Maginnis (1867-1955) and Timothy Walsh (1868-1934) of Boston. Their skill in ecclesiastical design was evident in scores of Catholic churches across the United States, including the National Shrine of the Immaculate Conception in Washington, D.C. Their loss to Masqueray in the competition of 1904 was balanced by the commission, which they accepted in the Spring of 1923, to design a rectory and sacristy, and to produce plans for the completion of the interior. Work on the rectory began in March 1924. The residence was ready for occupancy shortly before Christmas.

Concurrent with the construction of the rectory was the building of the sacristy, carried out by Foley Brothers of St. Paul. The addition of the octagonal structure to the rear of the Cathedral altered and softened Masqueray's original concept, which had ended too abruptly with the apsidal chapels.[13] Yet in another way it reinforced that concept, for, with its copper dome and spacious interior, it was a smaller version of the Cathedral which it served. The walls were of Briar Hill stone, quarried in Ohio (figs. 6.7, 6.8). Atop the dome stood an angel, the creation of Ernest Pellegrini of New York; facing the apse, the graceful heavenly visitor showed deep reverence as it gazed upon the sanctuary of the Lord (fig. 6.9). Under the dome stood a series of richly carved, dark oak consoles and closets (fig. 6.10). In raised stone panels imbedded within the piers and over the sanctuary door were carved quota-

6.7 The Sacristy, 1924

tions (in Latin) from the psalms. All refer rather appropriately to the joy experienced by priests as they prepare to offer sacrifice to God.[14] Around the base of the dome, and also in Latin, were placed the prophetic words of Ezekiel 43:4-5, "And the glory of the Lord entered the temple by way of the gate which faces the east, but spirit lifted me up and brought me to the inner court. And I saw that the temple was filled with the glory of the Lord" (fig. 6.11). The sacristy was completed on May 17, 1925. Public reaction to it was favorable, for, as Ryan explained, it was "a masterpiece quite in keeping with the great Cathedral."[15]

In their plans for the decoration of the Cathedral's interior, Maginnis and Walsh were careful not to venture beyond the guidelines established by Masqueray two decades earlier. Between 1925 and 1931 they completed on paper all of the details — an enormous task, considering that up to that point only the ceiling of the apse, Warren's baldachin, and Masqueray's three chapels had been finished. For once, funding was not a problem. On February 26, 1922, a campaign to complete the interior

6.8 The Sacristy. Detail of the Exterior Decoration

had been announced. For the first time, Cathedral parishioners had been given weekly collection envelopes. They had been asked to donate one hour's wages each week, and the general response was enthusiastic.

Embellishment of the Sanctuary

The sanctuary and the apsidal chapels were the first large spaces completed. Plans for their embellishment were completed in June 1925. Contracts for the materials were awarded the following month. The setting of the stone and marble began in December, and continued over eighteen months of "noise, dust and disorder," until May 7, 1927.[16] The inconvenience was soon forgotten as Maginnis and Walsh's design was realized, for it proved to be a fitting accompaniment to Warren's altar and canopy. Within the sanctuary the two Bostonians resorted to a potpourri of dazzling marbles, in keeping with the only decorative scheme already there: the expansive and brightly colored representation of the Holy Spirit and His Seven Gifts, painted on the ceiling by Pennell, Gibbs, and Quiring of Boston, some seven years earlier (fig. 6.12; from left to right, the figures in the coffers above the windows symbolize knowledge, counsel, understanding, piety, wisdom, fear of the Lord, and fortitude.) For the curving steps forming the base of the main altar, they used Istrian

6.9 The Sacristy. Angel in Prayer

marble. To enliven the Alpine green floor, with its Botticino border, they added diamond-shaped insets of Levanto Red, framed by Swiss Cipollino. In the middle of the arrangement was laid a bronze shield containing the coat of arms of the Archdiocese of St. Paul, surrounded by Sylvan Green and Levanto Red (fig. 6.13). The shield was donated by Rose Ann O'Connell, who for over thirty years served as cook to the McConville family, itself among the most generous donors to the Cathedral. Five steps below the sanctuary floor ran the altar railing, its posts of Portora Black and rails of Botticino interrupted only by the central bronze gates, bearing the traditional symbols of the chalice, wheat, and grapes. Finally, eight columns of Botticino were positioned between the arches separating the sanctuary from the ambulatory chapels; above the columns were inserted oval-shaped pieces of Verona Red and Greek Tinos marble.

The choir stalls, designed to hold one hundred voices, were made of dark American walnut and followed the curve of the sanctuary (fig. 6.14). In the midst of the rich ornamentation, they provided a touch of simplicity, for their sole decoration was a conventional border around the front and back of each stall. Planted on the Epistle side of the sanctuary, the twelve-foot-high circular pulpit of white cream marble was decorated by Albert H. Atkins (d.1951) of Boston (fig. 6.15). Beneath its reading desk was carved an oval cartouche, the flat tones of which contrasted with its highly polished background. On its octagonal base were placed portraits of the four evangelists, with that of St. John, the "Beloved Disciple," facing the nave.

The Grilles

Atkins' decoration of the pulpit coincided with his work on what many consider to be the finest piece of art in the Cathedral: the bronze *Te Deum* and *Magnificat* grilles located between the piers at the back of the sanctuary (fig. 6.16).[17] Two years were spent in their design and subsequent execution by the Twin City Ornamental Iron and Bronze Company of Minneapolis. The seven grilles, each measuring 21'6" by 9'10" and composed of two panels joined by bronze molding, were installed in 1926. Though intended to serve a practical purpose, separating

6.10 The Sacristy. Detail of the Cabinets

6.11 The Sacristy. Interior of the Dome

6.12 The Sanctuary Apse. The Seven Gifts of the Holy Spirit

6.13 The Bronze Shield in the Sanctuary Containing the Archdiocesan Coat of Arms

the sanctuary from the apsidal chapels and providing a fitting background for the altar, their major impact was symbolic. "Books in bronze," they portray humanity's response to God's grace. Among the holy men and women illustrated, special recognition is given to the patron saint of the Cathedral. Each grille is surmounted by a life-size

frieze re-creating a major event in the life of St. Paul (fig. 6.17). The story unfolds from left to right: Paul's conversion, his appearance before Sergius Paulus, his miracles and preaching at Lystra, the closing of the Council of Jerusalem, his work in Athens, his stormy visit to Ephesus, and martyrdom. Above each of the frieze panels is the "shield of faith"; the sword forming the central motif is the age-old symbol of the Apostle to the Gentiles, who wrote, "...the sword of the spirit...[is]...the Word of God" (Ephesians 6:17). Under each panel are four tiers of medallions, the lowest of which, bedecked with singing angels, is situated directly behind the choir stalls. The upper three sets of medallions represent, once again from left to right, the prophets (Melchizedek, David, and John the Baptist; Abraham, Moses, and Isaiah), apostles (Philip, Andrew, Simon and Jude; Peter, Thomas, James and John), martyrs (Ignatius of Antioch, Cyprian of Carthage, and Lawrence; Stephen, Justin, and Cornelius), the joys and sorrows of the Virgin Mary (the Visitation, the finding of Jesus in the Temple, and the Sorrowful Mother; the Annunciation, the Presentation, and Mary and Joseph), virgins and martyrs (Agnes, Catherine of Siena, and Elizabeth of Hungary; Agatha, Anastasia, and Joan of

6.14 The Choir Stalls

6.15 The Pulpit

6.16 *The* Te Deum *Grilles. Panels I-III (South Side of the Ambulatory)*
The friezes at the top show scenes from the life of St. Paul (*left to right:* his conversion, appearance before Sergius Paulus, and work at Lystra).

Arc), Doctors of the Church (Augustine, Leo, and Thomas Aquinas; Ambrose, Gregory, and Bernard), and founders and confessors (Dominic, Vincent de Paul, and Edward the Confessor; Benedict, John Baptist de la Salle, and Louis IX of France). Surrounding all eight medallions in each grille are scores of graceful floral designs, Renaissance rosettes, and cherubs with outspread wings. The consummate artistry of the ensemble becomes most apparent when one looks at its dozens of faces (fig. 6.18). Each is original, distinct, and different from traditional renditions of the particular person. Moreover, all the characters, while sacred, are convincingly human. Paralleling Atkins' flawless artistry was his virtuosity. The

6.17 *The* Te Deum *Grilles. Panel V (North Side of the Ambulatory)*
Top to bottom: Paul's preaching at Athens, Sts. Agnes and Agatha, Sts. Catherine of Siena and Anastasia, Sts. Elizabeth of Hungary and Joan of Arc, and the Angelic Choir.

grilles are exactly the same on both sides: every face, ornament, and symbol is identical on the reverse side. Consequently, there is no "right" or "wrong" way to read their message. All their features are cast in silhouette and appear three-dimensional. Few, indeed, are the American cathedrals which can boast of an ecclesiastical work of such a scale or spirit.

The Shrines of the Nations

Behind the grilles lay the six apsidal chapels, completed between 1926 and 1928. As early as 1905 these alcoves had been earmarked to serve as the Shrines of the Nations, honoring the "apostles and spiritual fathers" of those races which had played a large role in the settlement of Minnesota. The six original choices, as announced by Archbishop Ireland, had been St. Patrick, for the Irish; St. Austin, for the Anglo-Saxons; St. Remy, for the French; St. Boniface, for the Germans; Sts. Cyril and Methodius, for the Slavs; and St. Ansgar, for the Scandinavians.[18] Yet by the time of execution, some twenty years later, three of the saints — Austin, Remy, and Ansgar — had been supplanted by St. John the Baptist, for the French Canadians; St. Anthony of Padua, for the Italians; and St. Therese of Lisieux, protectress of all the missions.[19] The chapels' main walls were covered with Botticino marble. Distinguishing each chapel was the ornamental use of marble imported from the country of the saint whose shrine it was. This marble was used for the panel behind the statue of the patron, the altar frontal, and, in unpolished form, the large rondelle embedded within the Alpine green and white marble floor in front of each chapel. Each presented a fascinating variety of colors and textures, which was sharpened by the different designs and workmanship of each of the six statues. Their only real similarities were in material and point of origin: they were all of Trani marble, and were carved in Italy, from models sent by the various sculptors.

The chapel of St. Patrick was the first completed, and dedicated on March 17, 1928 (fig. 6.19). The statue of the saint, designed by Sidney W. Woollett of Boston, was blessed by Msgr. Patrick O'Neill, in the presence of the Ancient Order of Hibernians and its Ladies Auxiliary. Symbolic of the Christianization of Ireland was the use of sea green Connemara marble, the carving of the Gospel book and shamrock upon the pedestal of the statue, and the prominently placed quotation (in Latin) of Patrick's fondest wish for his converts, "That you may be Roman just as you are Christian."

The dedication of the chapel of St. Boniface occurred on June 3, 1928 (fig. 6.20). The ceremony, featuring sermons in both English and German, was preceded by a large parade. The statue of the saint was the work of

Albert H. Atkins. On the front of the altar was inscribed in Latin, "Missionary of St. Peter." The surrounding decorative marble was German Formosa. Two weeks later, at another bilingual gathering, Archbishop Dowling presented the chapel of St. Anthony to the Italians of the Archdiocese (fig. 6.21). Once again, the sculptor was Atkins. On the front of the altar ran the salutation of a letter sent to the learned miracle-worker of Padua by his spiritual father, St. Francis of Assisi: "To Brother Anthony,

6.18 The Te Deum Grilles. Detail of Panel II (North Side of the Ambulatory) Sts. James and John.

my bishop." The ornamental panels were of Sienna Gray; in the middle of the altar frontal was a cherub-adorned inset.

On July 1, 1928, French families in the Archdiocese gathered for the dedication of the chapel of St. John the Baptist (fig. 6.22). Msgr. Ryan preached the sermon in English, and Father Paul Rulquin, pastor of St. Louis Church, St. Paul, its counterpart in French. Inspired by the moment when John identified Jesus — "Behold the Lamb of God" (John 1:29) — Atkins created the quintessential image of the missionary in the wilderness as a tribute to those priests whose zeal had brought them to the primitive Northwest territory. Behind the powerful statue, as well as on the front of the altar, rests a large slab of Swiss Cipollino.

On July 8, three thousand Minnesotans of Slavic origin witnessed the blessing of the statues of Sts. Cyril and Methodius (fig. 6.23). Father Joseph Cieminski

6.19 The Shrine of St. Patrick, 1926-1928

6.20 The Shrine of St. Boniface, 1926-1928

6.21 The Shrine of St. Anthony, 1926-1928

6.22 The Shrine of St. John the Baptist, 1926-1928

PRISCA VOS SLAVIS OPVS
EST DATORES DONA TVERI

6.23 The Shrine of Sts. Cyril and Methodius, 1926-1928

6.24 The Shrine of St. Therese of Lisieux, 1926-1928

preached in Polish. Father Emil Polasek, whose brother, Alban (1879-1965), had designed the memorial to the missionaries, preached in Bohemian. The chapel was highlighted by panels of St. Genevieve golden vein marble. Inscribed on the front of the altar was an excerpt from the Latin poetry of Leo XIII: "It is necessary for the Slavs that you, the givers, watch over the venerable, ancient, and old-fashioned gifts."

The last dedicated was the Shrine of St. Therese of Lisieux, on September 30, 1928 (fig. 6.24). Although the chapel was an exaltation of the personal sanctity of the "Little Flower,"[20] whose statue was the work of Atkins, it also reminded visitors of the heroism of another Frenchwoman. Set in the wall on the left side was a stone from the dungeon of Rouen, in which Joan of Arc was imprisoned during her trial. It had been sent to Archbishop Ireland in 1917 by George Frederick Kunz, President of the American Scenic and Historic Preservation Society.[21] The gift was made in recognition of Ireland's lifelong devotion to the saint whom he had once called, "the embodiment of patriotism and of religion," and the "most sweet, most beautiful, most sublime figure of womanhood known to history, save the Virgin Mother of Nazareth alone."[22] The undressed surface of the stone contrasted sharply with the surrounding French rosata ornamentation.

Tying these six chapels together was the ambulatory (fig. 6.25); its ceiling, finished in brick, was deeply vaulted in line with the emphatic verticality of the entire Cathedral. Midway in the passage, a hand-carved walnut screen, in conventional fleur-de-lis design, was positioned above the entrance to the sacristy (fig. 6.26). Its main purpose was to mask the chambers for the chancel organ, but with its burnished gold highlighting, it also added a note of ornamental detail to the area.

Though the Shrines of the Nations are small — each is only thirteen by fifteen feet — and occupy perhaps the least conspicuous part of the edifice, their significance should not be underrated. Like the sculpture of the facade, they point to an important truth: that the Church's most glorious progress has come through the untiring commitment and repeated sacrifices of her missionaries. The chapels were meant to be celebrations in stone and marble of hundreds of years of evangelization, making the Cathedral "the Church of the Christian apostolate — as suggested by the name of its patron, St. Paul."[23] But the Shrines also are expressions of gratitude to God from the people to whom their patrons were sent. To emphasize this, both Ireland and Dowling insisted that the funds for the construction of each chapel come either entirely or at least in large part from the race or nationality represented therein. (The cost of each setting was approximately

6.25 The Ambulatory

$20,000.) In lieu of a donors' inscription, a parchment volume, listing the names of contributors, was placed within each altar.[24]

The years which saw the decoration of the apsidal chapels also witnessed the placing of the stonework on the four great piers supporting the dome. The last panel was set on February 15, 1927. The beauty and craftsmanship of the finished product only served to underscore the poignancy of the remaining whitewashed walls of the nave and transepts. Accordingly, in November 1929, Maginnis and Walsh were authorized to draw up plans for comple-

6.26 The Organ Screen over the Sacristy Entrance

tion of the interior. Two tasks were not included in this commission: the decoration of the dome, and the design and production of the stained glass windows. These were reserved for specialists. Maginnis and Walsh's scheme was approved in March 1931, and bids opened.

Barely underway, the effort was seriously hampered by two unexpected tragedies: the Great Depression and the death of Archbishop Dowling on November 28, 1930. The new Ordinary, John Gregory Murray, former Bishop of Portland (Maine), was installed in the scaffold-ridden Cathedral on January 27, 1932 (fig. 6.27). Unlike his

6.27 Archbishop John Gregory Murray

predecessors, Murray never worked out a general plan for the building, preferring to move toward its completion one step at a time. This piecemeal approach was nonetheless rooted in a sincerity and a sense of duty as profound as those displayed by Ireland and Dowling. In the long run, the "good Archbishop Murray" could point to a number of major additions and refinements as his legacy to the edifice.

The Chapel of the Sacred Heart

Chief among these was the embellishment of the chapel of the Sacred Heart, which had been included in Maginnis and Walsh's final design of 1931. Originally built to honor St. Paul, its patronage was reassigned by Ireland, who believed that a Pauline chapel in a Pauline cathedral was redundant. The placement of the marble began in November 1931, providing much needed employment. The marble was purchased from the Drake Marble and Tile Company of Minneapolis, for but a fraction of its original price. Due to the economic crisis, there was an

enormous overload of foreign stone sitting idle on New York docks. The project proceeded at a remarkably steady pace: the ceiling was completed in February 1932, and the rest of the chapel in early March. The statue of Jesus, sculpted of Trani marble by Woollett, was installed in July 1933. It was the gift of Mrs. J. B. Morehead.

In terms of spiritual and artistic effects, the chapel of the Sacred Heart was on a par with its three older sisters (fig. 6.28). Its main walls were of *Laredo Chiaro,* from Italy; the altar and columns, of Numidian Cipollino; the altar frontal, of Numidian Crimson; and the retable, of dark Botticino. Behind the statue stood a panel of *Rojo Alicante*, from Spain; the oval on the base and rectangles above were of Morocco Red onyx. The sense of sharply contrasting colors and tints was intensified by the green Tinos floor, from Greece, and the rail of Portora Black and light Botticino. Around the apse, in Latin, was inscribed the opening words of the entrance antiphon for the Mass of the Sacred Heart: "The thoughts of His heart are to all generations" (Psalm 33:11). The symbol of the loving heart, enshrined within this majestic setting, may be seen as two-edged: the funds for the chapel were easily raised by popular subscription, but at a time when many Minnesotans had very little.

Dressing the Nave and Transepts

As the chapel of the Sacred Heart neared completion, work began on the interior walls of the nave and transepts (fig. 6.29). At their base was installed a seven-foot-high wainscot of polished French Tavernelle marble. The upper sections, contracted to the C. H. Young Company, were covered by a six- inch-thick veneer of golden buff Mankato stone, which was affixed to the brick wall through a layer of insulating hollow tiles. The selection of Mankato stone, or American Travertine, as it is sometimes called, was neither easy nor quick. According to Msgr. Ryan, the decision was made only after much study, travel, and experimentation.[25] Samples of various stones were set on the Cathedral walls, and several engineers were consulted. The final choice was based upon a number of considerations, some practical, some acoustical, and some aesthetic. Durability, tensile strength, and availability were undoubtedly the most formidable advantages of Travertine, in addition to its seven shades of buff, which complemented the colored marbles of the chapels, and its easy response to delicate carving. The pegging of the stone continued uninterrupted through 1934. Whether alone, or, as in the transepts, combined with the marble columns of the balustrades, the Travertine does exactly what its selectors had hoped: it assists the walls in supporting the extremely heavy dome and roof, while

6.28 The Chapel of the Sacred Heart, 1931-1933

6.29 The Unfinished Interior as seen during the Installation of Austin Dowling as Second Archbishop of St. Paul, March 25, 1919
The bunting and greenery did little to mitigate the starkness of the whitewashed brick walls and the uncolored glass in the Shrines of the Nations. Still in use were the main altar and the episcopal chair from the third Cathedral.

inspiring on the inside a warmth, variety, and beauty conducive to a prayerful attitude. Concerning the latter achievement, Ryan provides an interesting comment. After the transformation, he was besieged by delighted parishioners, telling him, "now we can pray and worship better."[26]

Shortly after 1935, and in keeping with the didactic nature of the edifice, Scriptural verses in English were inscribed on the walls of the transepts. Along the balustrade in the left transept is an admonition: "Holy this. None other than the house of God and the gate of

heaven"(Genesis 28:17). The lintels of each door, on the other hand, carry prayers. Above the upper door is, "Conduct me, O Lord, in Thy way and I will walk in Thy truth" (Psalm 86:11). Above the lower is, "Direct me in Thy truth and teach me, for Thou art God my Saviour" (Psalm 25:5). The themes of the verses in the right transept parallel those of their counterparts on the other side of the church. The balustrade quotation is taken from Revelation 21:3, "Behold the tabernacle of God with men and He will dwell with them." The lintel of the upper door reads, "May the Lord keep thy coming in and thy going out now and forever" (Psalm 120:8). That of the lower is excerpted from the Sermon on the Mount: "So let your light shine before men that they may see your good works" (Matthew 5:16).

Vestibules and Narthex

During the completion of the interior, work also began on the four side vestibules. The walls were sided with green Tinos, a Greek marble of so soothing a color and texture that it naturally instills in the arriving (and perhaps harried) worshiper that sense of calmness and reverence necessary in the House of God. On the wall of the upper vestibule of the left transept is a commemoration of Cardinal Vannutelli's placement of the adjoining lintel in 1910. All four areas were completed and reopened to the public in August 1934.

The decoration of the sixty-two-by-sixteen-foot narthex, including its two side chapels, required a full five years (1937-1942) (fig. 6.30). Its walls were finished in

Italian *Verde Antico*, and its floor, in Tennessee Pink marble. At its southern end, behind a heavily ornamented wrought-iron grille, was the baptistry, sixteen feet square, its lining of Numidian Cipollino and dark Botticino (fig. 6.31). The font, of light Botticino, stood out dramatically against the darker walls. At the northern end of the narthex was planned a Founders' Chapel, of the same size and materials as the baptistry. The purpose of this specially reserved area was outlined long before construction of the Cathedral had even begun:

> Large volumes, so large that they can never be mislaid or lost, are being prepared, proof in paper and in binding against the ravages of time, the pages of which will record the names and the addresses of all contributors together with the sums contributed, and the sums paid. Those volumes will be preserved in fire-proof castings in a chapel of the Cathedral to be called 'The Founders' Chapel.' Over the gateway to this

6.30 The Narthex looking north

6.31 The Baptistry

chapel a metallic scroll will announce that for all time to come, on the Thursday morning of every week, mass will be celebrated for the spiritual health and welfare of all, living or dead, whose names are there preserved.[27]

One large memorial volume was produced, at a cost of $400, by the end of 1916. The work, commended by the Executive Building Committee for its excellent penman-

6.32 Title Page of the Memorial Volume in the Founders' Chapel

ship and beautiful design, remains to this day in the chapel (fig. 6.32).[28] It is a fascinating compilation; every donor, regardless of the size of his or her contribution, is listed. Consequently, the amounts range from several thousand dollars to a few cents (fig. 6.33). Above the volume, on the western wall, are lists of the Bishops and Archbishops of St. Paul and the rectors of the Cathedral.[29]

Of course, not all of the architectural and decorative transformations of the first Ryan era were on a grand scale. New confessionals were added in September and October 1935. In 1940, in preparation for the Ninth National Eucharistic Congress, Archbishop Murray ordered significant additions to the main altar. With the installation of a gradine and the retirement of the Slade altar set, an entirely new effect was created, one which included larger candlesticks and an over life-size crucifix.

The Cathedral, object of so much attention and artistry during the twenty-five years of Msgr. Ryan, was also at the same time host to several unforgettable ceremonies. The first of many ordinations within its walls occurred on June 9, 1930. On October 27, 1936, Eugenio Cardinal Pacelli, Vatican Secretary of State, celebrated

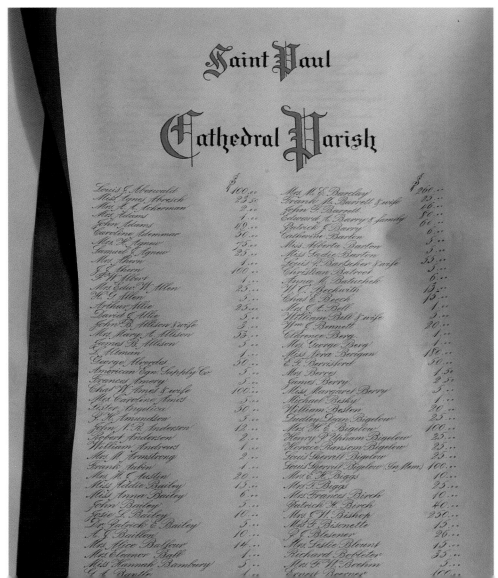

6.33 A Typical Page from the Memorial Volume in the Founders' Chapel

6.34 Cardinal Pacelli at the Cathedral of Saint Paul, October 27, 1936.
To the right is his host, Archbishop Murray

Mass and addressed the overflow crowd (fig. 6.34). The impression made by the building upon the future Pius XII was not recorded, but one of his travelling companions, Count Enrico Galeazzi, a noted Roman architect, was so stunned by its size and beauty that he spent almost his entire time in St. Paul studying it.[30] And in June 1941 the Cathedral served as the site for the religious reception of Dennis Cardinal Dougherty, Archbishop of Philadelphia, who had come to the Twin Cities as papal legate to the Ninth National Eucharistic Congress.

By 1940, the year of Lawrence Ryan's resignation, the Cathedral of St. Paul was substantially complete. A few tasks remained, but these seemed minimal compared to the scope and challenge of the work so efficiently supervised by Ryan and so expertly executed by his designers and craftsmen. Further additions and refinements of the interior would be made after 1940, but none of these would mitigate the truth of the observation that while the exterior belonged in a special way to Ireland, the interior belonged, in an equally special way, to Ryan.

Chapter Seven

Motherhood: Home of a Spiritual Family

Overleaf: **The Lamb of God.** *Detail from the East Rose Window*

Spectacular though it was, the work of Warren, Maginnis and Walsh, and Atkins comprised but one part of the interior decorative scheme executed during the Cathedral's first three decades. Simultaneous with the installation of the baldachin, wainscoting, and grilles, was the placement of the stained glass, along with an assortment of paintings and statuary. Balancing these aesthetic endeavors were a number of practical concerns, for without proper heating, lighting, and sound systems, worshipers would be hard-pressed to feel inspired by the surrounding artistry. Thus, during and after the first Ryan era, engineers and acoustical analysts, operating deep under the floor and within the walls of the edifice, worked side-by-side with the designers and carvers. Their collaboration produced an atmosphere of comfort blended with overall grandeur, to create a structure attuned as fully to the simple needs of prayerful men and women as to the desire to honor God in a monumental way.

The Stained Glass

In a building filled with many outstanding examples of twentieth-century American ecclesiastical art, the stained glass windows are regarded by many as their crowning glory. Though designed and placed by several different glassworkers over a period of thirty years, these colored panels share a consistently high sense of line, color, and workmanship; from Millet's windows in the chapels, to Pickel's in the sacristy, the quality remains remarkably even. Differences of style and content notwithstanding, they form a harmonious ensemble.

Millet and the Chapel Windows

The earliest glass panels installed in the Cathedral were those in the chapels of St. Peter, St. Joseph, and the Blessed Virgin, executed between 1917 and 1920. Their creator, Louis J. Millet (1856-1923) of Chicago, produced in each shrine an ensemble in keeping with the Cathedral's decorative scheme, as laid out by his friend and former classmate at the Beaux-Arts, Masqueray.[1] The subjects are monumental in form and solemn in rendition: their pronounced colors add greater variety to the wide array of tones in the surrounding marble. Like their neighboring works in stone and stucco, the windows in the chapel of St. Peter point to the Divine institution of the Papacy. Over the Gospel side of the altar stands a predominantly light blue and coral panel of St. Peter, the first Pope; over the Epistle side, a rather lifelike portrait in primarily dark blue and gold, of Benedict XV (1914-1922), his two-hundred-and-fifty-ninth successor (fig. 7.1). Thus is set in glass the belief in the unbroken line of Roman Pontiffs, who trace their authority to the commission given by Christ.

Four windows in the chapel of St. Joseph extol the virtues of Jesus' foster father. To the left of the apse in the first opening, is a plant, above which is a lamp, symbol of spiritual enlightenment, and under which is etched the Latin rendition of Luke 12:42, "Behold the faithful and

7.1 The Chapel of St. Peter. St. Peter and Benedict XV

prudent servant whom the master sets over his servants." Within the second opening grows a stately palm, framed by the scales of justice at the top, and the responsorial verse of the Divine Office in honor of a saint: "The Lord leads the just man through the paths of truth and will show him the Kingdom of God." To the right of the apse, in the third opening, stands an oak around which is ribboned the responsorial verse of the Divine Office of St. Joseph: "God made him the master of His household and gave him charge over all His possessions." Above the oak hangs a sword, emblem of fortitude. Also from the Office of the Saint is the inscription accompanying a vase of lilies in the fourth opening: "The just man shall blossom like the lily; he shall flourish forever in the courts of our God." Above this scene is suspended an hourglass, a practical reminder that humanity's stay on earth is indeed short, and ought to be lived with a constant view toward heaven.

Celebrated in the four windows of the Marian chapel

7.2 The Chapel of the Blessed Virgin Mary. The Crucifixion

7.3 The Shrines of the Nations. St. Clare

are the key events in the Virgin's life. Under the representation of each event is placed either a brief description or a prayer: the Annunciation ("The Angel of the Lord appeared to Mary, and she conceived of the Holy Spirit"), the Nativity ("Holy Mother of God, Virgin Mary, pray for us to the Lord our God"), the Death of Jesus ("Queen of Martyrs, pray for us, you who stood next to the Cross of Jesus") (fig. 7.2), and the Assumption ("Mary is assumed into heaven"). Of these four only the last follows a clearly traditional iconography, being a close copy of the famous painting by the seventeenth- century Spanish master, Bartolomé Esteban Murillo.

La Farge and the Shrines of the Nations

Nearly a decade passed before the installation of the next series of stained glass, that in the Shrines of the Nations, executed by Bancel La Farge in 1927-1928. Son of the celebrated painter, in whose studio he had served as an assistant toward the close of the nineteenth century, Bancel (1865-1938) worked successfully in a wide variety of artistic media, including oils, mosaics, watercolors, and pastels. The depth of his talent, however, was most strikingly revealed through his stained glass, which continued and refined the practice of deep-toned opalescence introduced by his father. (The opaque particles in opalescent glass scatter the light, so as to create different levels of transparency within the same pane of glass. The resulting three-dimensional effect, though subtle, is nevertheless quite real, and highly dramatic.) To his creations the

7.4 The Shrines of the Nations. St. Columbin   *7.5 The Shrines of the Nations.* St. Bridget   *7.6 The Shrines of the Nations.* St. Wenceslaus

younger La Farge brought not only the meticulous craftsmanship assimilated during twelve years of training in France and Italy, but also a devout Catholicism, which made him one of the most prominent and widely respected laymen in the early twentieth-century American Church. In addition to his membership on the Board of Trustees of Albertus Magnus College, New Haven, and on the advisory board of *Commonweal,* he served as President of the Liturgical Arts Society of America from 1935 to 1938. While he produced works with secular themes, he spent most of his career portraying religious subjects for Protestant as well as Catholic churches throughout the United States.

La Farge received the commission for the apsidal windows in 1926. Though based on his growing national reputation, his selection also contained a personal note: as

a young boy in Newport, Rhode Island, La Farge had befriended the son of a butler in a neighboring mansion. Fifty years later, the butler's son, now Archbishop Dowling of St. Paul, chose his former playmate to execute the twelve windows honoring heroic men and women of Scripture and Church history.[2]

To frame the altar in each of the six chapels, La Farge and his son Thomas designed two slender panels representing secondary patron saints of the nationality for whom each chapel was constructed. Thus, along the southern half of the ambulatory, the shrine of St. Anthony is bordered by windows memorializing two other models of Franciscan holiness among the Italian people, Saints Francis and Clare (fig. 7.3); that of St. John the Baptist, by Saints Zachary (John's father) and Simeon (the prophet of Luke 2:25-35); and that of St. Patrick, by Saints Columbin (521-597), the founder of monasteries in England and Brittany (fig. 7.4), and Bridget (453-523), the foundress of Irish conventual life (fig. 7.5). Along the northern half, the chapel of St. Boniface includes images of Saints Bruno (1030-1101), founder of the Carthusian order, and Gertrude (1255-1301/2), the greatest exponent of medieval Benedictine mysticism; that of Saints Cyril and Methodius, through Saints Stanislaus (c. 1030-1097), Polish bishop and martyr, and Wenceslaus (905-935), the martyred Bohemian ruler (fig. 7.6); and that of St. Therese, through her fellow Carmelites, Saints Teresa of Avila (1515-1582) and John of the Cross (1542-1591), the two most powerful personalities of the Spanish Counter-Reformation. Under La Farge's supervision , the windows were executed by the New York firm of Otto Heinigke, which had worked with the elder La Farge earlier in the century. The last of the panels was placed on December 14, 1928.

Public and critical reaction to the ensemble was so positive that La Farge was immediately given the contract for the windows of the Sacred Heart chapel, the general design of which had recently been unveiled by Maginnis and Walsh. Once again, his close collaboration with the Boston architects inspired him to produce two panels not only iconographically but also aesthetically synchronized with the vibrant array of marbles celebrating the mercy and compassion of the Savior. To the left of the altar is a representation of Jesus as the Bread of Life. Sitting at the Eucharistic table, He blesses those who approach to partake of the banquet, the main features of which — the host and the wine — are found at the bottom of the composition. To the right of the altar the companion panel presents the Tree of Life, before which stands a radiant Jesus; in the shade of the bounteous tree a deer grazes. But the serenity of the scene is broken further down by the image of a heart pierced seven times, a reminder that salvation and suffering are inextricably linked: by the wounds of one would all others be healed (Isaiah 53:5). The windows were placed in 1932, and were received as enthusiastically as had been their apsidal counterparts a few years earlier.

Charles J. Connick

As La Farge prepared his final pieces for the Cathedral, Charles J. Connick prepared his first. Enlisting Connick was one of Archbishop Dowling's inspirations during his eleven- year administration. Regarded as the world's finest contemporary craftsman in stained glass, Connick (1875-1945) had already designed hundreds of windows and was well on his way to receiving every major award in his field. Professional societies vied for his membership, universities and colleges loaded him with honorary

degrees, and churches of all denominations deluged him with requests for glass settings. At his retirement Connick closed a career spanning four decades of distinguished work. From the windows of St. Patrick's and St. John the Divine, in New York, to those of Grace Cathedral in San Francisco, he had almost single- handedly brought about a rebirth of American ecclesiastical decoration. His work in the Cathedral of St. Paul was not his only legacy to Minnesota,[3] but it remains among the finest examples of that subtle blending of technical skill and artistic creativity through which he sought to re-create the glories of medieval stained glass.

Basing his views on first-hand study of European, and particularly French and English cathedrals, Connick emphasized that a craftsman in glass should strive to create "not...a picture made transparent but a window made rarely beautiful."[4] True beauty, as Connick learned during his study of Chartres Cathedral, was realized only through the interplay of light and color. Eschewing the modern era's fascination with opaque glass, he returned to the use of "antique" glass. The nearly transparent panes, when acted upon by brilliant light, assumed gleaming and vibrant patterns of vivid color, leaving in the viewer a sense of "other-worldliness and magic well-being."[5] Furthermore, as the direction and intensity of the light shifted through the day, the mood conveyed by the glass became stronger or subtler. In short, a stained glass window was a living entity, "a sensitive arrangement at the mercy of light."[6] Though painterly in its design, Connick's glass showed none of the static quality of a canvas. Though architectural in its setting, it resisted the immobility of neighboring pillars, cornices, and portals. According to Connick, if his craft showed an affinity to any of its sister arts, it was to music, for the rarely beautiful composition was the one which "sang" throughout the day, proclaiming the timelessness of the soul and universal longing for peace and beauty.

The Sanctuary Windows

Connick's artistic debut at the Cathedral of St. Paul came in seven sanctuary windows, which he and his associates designed during the late 1920s. Each window celebrates one of the sacraments, each of which is represented by a medallion held by a rainbow-borne Archangel.

Baptism is the subject of the first window on the left. Dominated by the color white, the traditional sign of purity, the panel features the Archangel Gabriel presenting the baptism of the Ethiopian eunuch by St. Philip (Acts 8:26-39). To its right stands the window of Confirmation, with its emphatic use of yellows and reds. The armor-bedecked Michael shows St. John the Evangelist in the act of confirming a youth, to the accompaniment of tongues of fire and golden rays (Acts 2:3). At left-center, the next window illustrates the Sacrament of Holy Orders. Purple, one of the symbols of ministry, is the dominant tone here. The Archangel Zadkiel holds a knife, his traditional emblem, and the representation of Christ commissioning the Apostles: "As the Father has sent me, so I send you" (John 20:21). Above, the Dove and a ray of light point to the unmistakable presence of the Holy Spirit. The center window extols the central feature of the Catholic faith, the Sacrament of the Eucharist (fig. 7.7). Its placement directly over the site of the tabernacle was deliberate. The Archangel Raphael, carrying a staff, gourd, and traveller's pouch, proffers a view of the Last Supper (Matthew 26:26). The predominance of the color green reflects the hope of salvation expressed by those who receive the Body and Blood of Christ. Matrimony is the subject of the window at right- center: the Archangel Jophiel, whose attribute is the flaming sword, bears a medallion with the bowed figures of Adam and Eve, joined together by the hand of God (Genesis 2:24). The window's primary color is blue. Second from the right is the heavily reddish representation of the Sacrament of Penance (fig. 7.8). The Archangel Uriel presents one of the most dramatic moments in the life of Jesus: His forgiveness of a sinful woman (Luke 7:44). To the far right is the commemoration of the Sacrament of Extreme Unction (now, the Anointing of the Sick). The composition is in violet; its funereal tone was considered natural by a pre-Vatican II Church which reserved this sign of God's grace exclusively for the dying. The Archangel Chamuel holds an urn and a tableau of the Apostles Peter, James and John in the process of anointing the sick (Mark 6:13).

Each window cost $1,400. Five of them were financed by private individuals: Annabel McQuillan (Baptism), Kathryn Manahan (Confirmation), Mr. and Mrs. David H. Ryan (Holy Orders), Katherine Prendergast (the Eucharist), and Mrs. William O'Brien (Matrimony). The windows representing Penance and Extreme Unction were donated by the women of the Altar and Rosary Societies, and the parishioners, respectively.

The East Rose Window

Connick's second commission was the east rose window (fig. 7.9). It was designed in 1931, with the assistance of Maginnis and Walsh. The glass arrived on April 6, 1932, and installation above the choir gallery began the next day. Total cost of the window, which was a memorial to Archbishop Dowling, was $18,000, paid for by the Cathedral parishioners. For Connick the opportunity to create so prominent a work of art in so majestic a setting was one to be relished. As he told the window's donors,

A great rose window is a glorious opportunity

7.7 (top) The Sanctuary. The Eucharist

7.8 (bottom) The Sanctuary. Penance

85

7.9 The Resurrection *(The East Rose Window)*

for the Craftsman who would express his vision of spiritual beauty in lyric color. The traditions that surround famous rose windows deepen the impression that their jewelled splendors are directly related to spiritual aspirations and emotions....

An eastern rose window has a special appeal of its own. Its response to the first light of the morning — gray, then rosy, and finally a full burst of sunlight, symbolizes a spiritual awakening day after day. So I delighted in the opportunity of designing and making the eastern rose window for the Cathedral of Saint Paul. I saw it at once in reds, golds, blues and whites alight

with the morning sun — the colors jostling each other in joyful rout like notes in music.[7]

The window's theme is the Resurrection, its inspirational text taken from John 1:4, "In Him was life, and the life was the light of men." At its center stands the Lamb of God holding aloft the banner of victory over death (see p. 79). Surrounding and supporting this venerable Paschal symbol are the twelve apostles. Saints Peter, Paul, James, and John, along with their respective symbols, are prominently featured (figs. 7.10, 7.11), while their eight colleagues form the arms of the cross. Woven through the background is the motif of the vine and branches, symbol of Christ and His followers. Entwined within the wide surrounding border is a foliated pattern, emphasizing that the Lamb of God is the center of all growth. In the small circles clustered around the window opening are representations of stars. Those with six points signify the Creation; those with five refer to the New Testament. In filling a space some twenty-six feet in diameter, Connick brought together faith and art in a combination of modern techniques with the spirit of medieval craftsmanship.

Shortly after the completion of the eastern rose window, Connick produced the lunette over the chapel of the Blessed Virgin. Not surprisingly, its theme was the Annunciation. The rendition within the dominating medallion is traditional: Mary, clothed in blue and white, kneels humbly before the Archangel Gabriel, who carries the lily of purity. The angelic salutation — "Hail Mary, full of grace, the Lord is with you" — forms part of the decorative border of the ruby- colored background of the

inspire. But while the window of the Resurrection appealed to the experience of the universal Church, those in the transepts presented the Christian message in the context of the unique American religious experience.

The South Rose Window

The theme of the southern window is the Beatitudes, as taught by Christ and exemplified by the lives of holy men and women of the New World (fig. 7.12). In its center stands Christ, robed in red and white, the colors of Divine love and purity, and holding an eight-pointed cross. Around Him are grouped members of all races, whose acceptance of Christ's teaching is symbolized by the globe at His feet. The scene is enclosed within a border of pomegranates, a sign of the Church's unity and universality. Revolving around this re-creation of the Sermon on the Mount are eight medallions. Each medallion is a tribute to a North or South American saint who imple-

7.10 St. James. *Detail from the East Rose Window*

7.11 St. John. *Detail from the East Rose Window*

medallion. Ribboning the entire field of glass is a richly decorated band of Marian symbols, including the fleur-de-lis, red-winged cherubim, and roses. Over the composition hovers the Holy Spirit in the form of a dove. The cost of the window was $3,000, which was raised quickly by the Girls' Sodality of the Blessed Virgin Mary. It was installed in 1932.

Due to other commitments, Connick was unable to provide designs for the rose windows of the transepts until 1939- 1940. The execution of the sketches, however, proceeded rapidly. The thousands of panes were set in place in mid- 1940. Like their sister to the East, the north and south roses sought to inform as well as please and

mented one of the Beatitudes in a particularly striking way. Surrounding these tributes is a richly symbolic field of clouds of pain, stars of hope, flames of religious zeal, and the growing vine. To reinforce the importance of these images, Connick used a combination of intense reds and blues throughout the area.

Representing the "poor in spirit" is St. Martin de Porres (1579-1639), a Dominican laybrother, who spent his life in the service of the underprivileged and oppressed of his native Lima. Doves, symbolic of those for whom he cared, pierce the border of the medallion. Martin's contemporary, and the first American to be canonized, St. Rose of Lima (1586-1617) is the exemplar of

7.12 The Beatitudes *(The South Rose Window)*

those who suffer persecution for justice's sake. Her spiritual trials are symbolized by demons shooting fiery darts (illness), carrying a scourge (penance), and whispering in her ear (temptation). The sword and palm, certifying a successful passage through a "dark night of the soul," stand close by. Peacemakers are honored through St. Toribio of Mogrovejo (1580-1606), Archbishop of Lima, who championed the rights of natives against Spanish oppression; next to his medallion rests an olive branch.

Blessed Catherine Tekakwitha (1656-1680) stands as the model for the "clean of heart" (fig. 7.13). Lilies bedeck the medallion of this Mohawk virgin and martyr who devoted her life to prayer, penance, and the care of the sick

and aged. The merciful are exalted through the ministry of St. Francis Solano (1549-1610), often called the "Wonder-worker of the New World." Francis fought pestilence in Spain and racism in South America. His compassion takes the form of a broken sword. Representative of those who hunger and thirst for justice is St. Frances Xavier Cabrini (1850-1917) (fig. 7.14). In a campaign to assist Italian immigrants in the Americas, she organized schools and founded hospitals. The accompanying sword and scales are a reminder of the tenacity of this foundress of the Missionary Sisters of the Sacred Heart. Those who mourn are bidden by Connick to study the life of St. Peter Claver (1581-1654), a Spanish Jesuit

7.13 Blessed Catherine Tekakwitha.
Detail from the South Rose Window

7.14 St. Frances Xavier Cabrini.
Detail from the South Rose Window

7.15 St. Peter Claver.
Detail from the South Rose Window

who labored among the Blacks of South America and the West Indies (fig. 7.15). To his right stands a slave dealer, along with the society women of Cartagena, who often chided the saint for caring too much about slaves. Along the side rises an inverted torch.

Finally, emblematic of the meek is St. Rose Philippine Duchesne (1769-1852), who brought the Society of the Sacred Heart to the United States. Near her is a reconstruction of her first foundation at St. Charles, Missouri. Looking on are the native Americans for whom she provided spiritual and physical comfort. Other symbols refer to Father Van Quickenbourne, the Jesuit missionary through whom she learned humility and patience, and to the ravages of yellow fever, which killed so many of her charges. Alongside these images rests a lamb, the essence of meekness. As a final touch, Connick interspersed eight nimbed doves along with a series of eight-pointed stars and eight-clustered grapes, around and among the medallions.

The North Rose Window

Recognizing that the north rose window would not enjoy the same exposure to light as its sister to the south, Connick used warmer tones to commemorate the eight American Jesuit Martyrs (fig. 7.16). At the center of the piece is Our Lady, Queen of Martyrs, attended by kneeling angels carrying palms of martyrdom (fig. 7.17). Under her feet is the globe, with the area of North America in which the eight ministered and died, colored deep red. As in the window of the Beatitudes, medallions contain representations and symbols of each martyr. St. John de Brébeuf (1593-1649) is portrayed at the moment of his death; boiling water is poured over his head, while red-hot hatchet blades are hung about his neck (fig. 7.18). Next to this scene of apparent defeat is one of triumph: the superstitious Iroquois forced him to paint the cross on his chapel white, believing it would end a drought. Having proven the futility of their belief, he repainted the

sign of faith red, and was rewarded with a thunderstorm. St. Gabriel Lalemant (1610-1649), who taught Iroquois children to pray, is pictured in the same martyrdom as his companion (fig. 7.19). In a third episode St. Noel Chabanel (1613-1649) is killed by a renegade Huron, while in a fourth St. René Goupil (1607-1642), laybrother and surgeon, is assaulted by Mohawks for showing their children how to make the Sign of the Cross. A burning chapel symbolizes the tragic end of the ministry of St. Charles Garnier (c. 1606-1649), while the equally gruesome demise of St. Anthony Daniel (1601-1648) is tempered by a glimpse of the missionary baptizing an entire tribe by aspersion. In adjacent settings, and forming a continuous narrative, St. Isaac Jogues (1607- 1646) is murdered as he enters the Iroquois council house. Nearby angels symbolize his dream of a heavenly choir assisting him at Mass. Counterbalancing this vision is the sight of one of his attackers fleeing with the priest's black box containing the religious books and liturgical items which the tribe considered bad magic. Attempting to recover Jogues' body, St. Jean Lalande (d. 1646), a young laybrother, is himself killed, as he steals forth from the house of a friendly Wolf tribesman.

Accentuating the field behind the medallions are the red roses of martyrdom. The small border of the window is highlighted with the pine branches and cones of the land sanctified by the eight Jesuits. Interspersed among the flora are renditions of native wild animals which often served as tribal symbols: the eagle, hawk, bear, moose, wolf, gopher, porcupine, and turtle (fig. 7.20). Finally, within the inner circles are golden stars with red rays and red-haloed doves, emblems of the spiritual wealth inherited by those who gladly sacrificed their lives for Christ.

From the day of their installation the north and south rose windows were acclaimed. There was consensus that their total cost of $30,000 was money well spent. Connick held a special affection for these creations during the final years of his life. Some months after their debut, he told

7.16 The American Jesuit Martyrs *(The North Rose Window)*

Msgr. Ryan, "I like to imagine what is happening to those rose windows in various weather, especially when snow is on the ground, for snow has its own way of influencing areas of stained glass, large or small."[8]

The Confessional Windows

Connick's death in 1945 did not end his guidance of the Cathedral's decorative scheme. In 1952, at a cost of $5,500, his associates designed the lunette over the chapel of St. Joseph (fig. 7.21). Portraying the Presentation of the infant Jesus in the Temple, it followed closely the spirit of Connick's artistry, as manifested in its companion piece over the Marian chapel executed twenty years earlier.

More ambitious was the creation of six windows for the transepts, installed in early 1953; their cost was $8,400. Since the two groups of panels are located above the confessionals, they share the same theme of forgiveness. In each, Christ, the source of all power, is flanked by windows showing a celebrated confessor and penitent. Under each of the figures rests an appropriate Scriptural verse in English.

On the south (Selby Avenue) side the central image is the Christ of Revelation, who gives to His Apostles the power of absolution: "Whose sins you shall forgive, they are forgiven them" (John 20:23) (fig. 7.22). The window, donated by Cathedral parishioners, is a memorial to Archbishop Ireland, whose episcopal crest appears in the

90

7.17 Mary, Queen of Martyrs.
Detail from the North Rose Window

7.18 The Death of St. John de Brébeuf.
Detail from the North Rose Window

7.19 The Death of St. Gabriel Lalemant.
Detail from the North Rose Window

7.20 A Bear.
Detail from the North Rose Window

7.21 The Chapel of St. Joseph. The Presentation

7.22 St. John Vianney, the Christ of Revelation, St. Mary Magdalene *(South Confessional Windows)*

area underneath Christ's feet. At Christ's left is St. Mary Magdalene (fig. 7.22), who carries the alabaster box of perfumes with which she anointed the Lord; its cover has fallen at her feet, near which is a brief explanation of the reason behind her act of gratitude: "Mary called Magdalen, out of whom seven devils were gone forth" (Luke 8:2). The window was the gift of the children of William P. and Margaret Kenney. At Christ's right stands St. John Vianney (1786-1859), wearing the violet stole of a confessor, a role for which he won international recognition during his own lifetime (fig. 7.22). Inscribed beneath him are the words of Jesus to the paralytic at Capernaum: "Be of good heart, thy sins are forgiven thee" (Matthew 9:2). The donors were Patrick and Mary Anne Butler.

In the middle of the north (Dayton Avenue) side is positioned a rendition of the Good Shepherd, given by Minnie Bell in memory of Bishop John J. Lawler, the first rector of the new Cathedral (fig. 7.23). His crest appears in the lower section with the words of John 10:11, "The Good Shepherd giveth His life for His sheep." To Christ's left is St. Dismas, the "Good Thief" of Calvary (fig. 7.23), whose dying plea to his neighbor is recorded: "Lord, remember me when Thou shall come into Thy Kingdom" (Luke 23:42). This striking reminder of Divine mercy was presented by Augustus Kennedy. To Christ's right is St. John Nepomucene (1345-1393), his finger upon his lips, a reference to his martyrdom for refusing to break the seal of the confessional (fig. 7.23). Beneath his feet is the Moldau river in Bohemia, into which he was thrown by

order of King Wenceslaus. Parallel to the river runs one of his favorite prayers: "Lord, set a guard upon my mouth. Post a sentry before my lips" (Psalm 141:3). The panel was donated by the family of Martin and Susan Kennedy.

During a quarter of a century, La Farge and Connick had set so high standard of creativity and technical skill that it might well have discouraged their lesser fêted colleagues from accepting the responsibility of completing the adornment of the windows. But this was not the case. In fact, the decade of the 1950s was in many ways the busiest and most productive period of glassworking in the Cathedral's history.

Unlike the large-scale efforts of the two earliest masters, the creations of Weston and Pickel were small in size, embellishing openings in the transepts, dome, narthex, and sacristy which had previously been overlooked. Differences in scale notwithstanding, the artistry of the Fifties was no less imaginative, richly symbolic, or deftly executed than that of the preceding twenty-five years.

Weston's Work in the Transepts and Narthex
In 1946 Chester A. Weston of Minneapolis was commissioned to design and fabricate panels for the remaining unadorned windows. Tremendously impressed by the work of the recently deceased Connick, Weston resolved to continue its medieval French flavor in his own creations, going so far as to import his glass from Europe. During some eleven years, he bedecked every major area of the edifice. The transept lunettes, bearing symbols

7.23 St. John Nepomucene, Christ the Good Shepherd, St. Dismas *(North Confessional Windows)*

of the Papacy (the tiara), hierarchy (the miter), clergy (the stole), and laity (the sword and urn), were installed in 1947.

In 1952, amid much publicity, the baptistry and Founders' Chapel were embellished with four windows depicting the history of the administration of the sacraments in the Archdiocese of St. Paul. Each of the sacraments is celebrated by a leading personality in the history of Minnesota Catholicism. As a tribute to the seven churchmen, their portraits are rather idealized. On the south wall of the baptistry is portrayed the first recorded baptism in the territory, performed on Antoinette, a dying Native American child, by Father Louis Hennepin in 1680. Sharing the window is a scene from yet another baptism, administered to a young Frenchman by a Jesuit priest in 1727 at Fort Beauharnois, near Frontenac. Each of these episodes carries an inscription in English: for the former, "That thou may havest life everlasting," taken from the baptismal ritual; and for the latter, "Unless a man be born again he cannot see the Kingdom of God" (John 3:3). At the top of the window are the Holy Spirit and a church, symbols of the graces imparted by the act of Christian initiation, while at the bottom lie the anchor (hope) and shell of baptism, along with the words, "Ego te baptizo." On the east wall of the baptistry is the celebration of Confirmation and Penance. In one frame Bishop Mathias Loras administers Confirmation during a pastoral visit to Mendota in 1839; underneath are inscribed the words of the rite: "May the Holy Spirit renew our souls, O Lord, by Thy Divine Sacrament." The second episode features Bishop Cretin hearing confession sometime in 1851; it is underscored by a variant of the words of absolution, "In Thy mercy, O Lord, grant us both pardon and peace." From the top of the window descends the Holy Spirit, symbol of Confirmation; at the bottom hang the keys of the Kingdom of God, evocative of Penance.

Extreme Unction and Holy Orders are the subjects of the east window of the Founders' Chapel. Illustrative of the first of these is Bishop Grace's anointing of a dying person in the presence of a nun who assists and answers the responses. Above this scene is a vial of holy oil; beneath it, the recommendation of James 5:14, "Let them pray over him, anointing him in the name of the Lord." Simultaneously, the young Bishop Ireland ordains a number of priests, with the words, "Bestow, Almighty Father, in these Thy servants the dignity of priesthood." Under this solemn rite are the stole, chalice, and book, the traditional clerical symbols. On the north wall of the Chapel Archbishop Dowling witnesses the sacrament of Matrimony (fig. 7.24), reminding the couple, "What God had joined together, let no man sunder" (Mark 10:9). The union of a man and women in Christ is represented by the cross and conjoined circles. Further down, Archbishop Murray shares the Eucharist with his congregation, using the pre-Vatican II formula of distribution, "May the Body of Our Lord Jesus Christ keep thy soul unto life everlasting." This greatest of all sacraments is also memorialized in the form of a cross and sheaf of wheat.

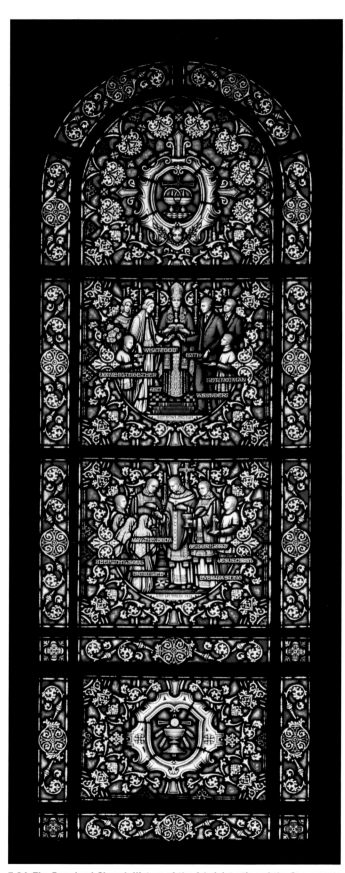

7.24 The Founders' Chapel. History of the Administration of the Sacraments in the Archdiocese of St. Paul: Matrimony and the Eucharist

In addition to the windows at either end of the narthex, Weston produced several smaller panes for the spaces above the main doors. Over the side portals he placed a simple Pauline motif of crosses and shields; above the central door rest the episcopal crests of the first five Ordinaries of St. Paul, with Bishop Cretin's most prominent. The cost of all the glass in the entrance area was borne completely by the Cathedral parishioners.

In 1953-1954, Weston capped the *succès d'estime* of the narthex with his installation of two equally ambitious series of windows in the main body of the Church. In the lower eastern walls of the transepts, he placed four panels representing the four groupings of members within the Body of Christ, a theme he repeated from his earlier lunettes. On the south side one finds St. Pius X (1835-1914), symbol of the Papacy (fig. 7.25), and his motto, "To restore all things in Christ" (Ephesians 1:10). Pius' companion in an adjacent piece, St. Anthony Mary Claret (1807- 1870), Archbishop of Santiago, Cuba, represents the episcopate (fig. 7.25). The intensity of his spiritual life is summarized in two citations. The first is derived from his own writings: "May God be known, loved and served by all." The second comes from his episcopal crest: "The love of Christ impels us" (2 Corinthians 5:14). On the north side stands St. John Bosco (1815-1888), representative of the clergy, accompanied by two passages: "What you do to the least of my brethren, you do unto me" (Matthew 25:40), and "Give me souls, take the rest" (his favorite prayer, a copy of which hung on the wall of his room). Symbolic of the laity, the fourth and final figure is St. Maria Goretti (1890-1902), whose commitment to virginity led to her death. The verses framing her refer to her simple virtue: "Blessed are the clean of heart" (Matthew 5:8), and "Had I but wings like a dove" (Psalm 55:7). Although these four modern examples of holiness were selected ostensibly because they represented different vocations within the Church, there undoubtedly was another consideration at play: all four were extremely popular among Catholics during the early 1950s. Being relatively close in time, they seemed more appealing as models; and their lives and ministries were especially well- known due to the fact that two of them (Claret and Goretti) were canonized in 1950, and a third (Pius X) in 1954. (Bosco had been added to the list of saints less than twenty years earlier, in 1934.)

The Windows in the Dome
Having completed his images of virtuous humanity, Weston turned to the representation of the angelic choirs of heaven. The twenty-four openings at the base of the dome, divided into eight groups of three windows, depict

the eight gradations of heavenly beings — Angels, Arch-angels, Virtues, Powers, Principalities, Dominations, Thrones, and Cherubim and Seraphim (fig. 7.26) — with each grouping in the traditional iconographic posture.[9] Blue serves as the dominant color for the panels portraying Angels and Principalities; green, for those featuring Virtues and Thrones; and red, for those containing Arch-angels, Dominations, Powers, and Cherubim and Seraphim. Repeated four times through the cycle is the encomium of Isaiah 6:3, "Holy, Holy, Holy, Lord God of hosts." Due to its rather high cost, the series was financed by the donations of non-parishioners as well as parishioners.

Pickel and the Sacristy Windows

The placement of the dome windows meant that the thirty- five-year process of glassworking in the Cathedral of St. Paul was at an end. Only the windows in Maginnis and Walsh's sacristy remained to be colored. These were turned over to Conrad Pickel, who designed and exe-

cuted seven pieces between 1959 and 1961. Born and raised in Germany, and now living in Florida, Pickel attempted to reproduce nature, but in his own "handwrit-ing." Though he had created glass for some one thousand churches and synagogues, he brought to every commis-sion a meticulousness learned during his days as an apprentice in the Munich Glassworks of Franz Mayer, at that time the largest stained glass shop in the world. His compositions for the sacristy in every way rival the larger pieces of Millet, Connick, La Farge, and Weston found in the main body of the church. While notably modern in their treatment of Christ the High Priest (the north wall) (fig. 7.27), the Immaculate Conception (the south wall) (fig. 7.28), episcopal functions and attire (the apse, to the west), and ecclesiastical symbols (the walls on either side of the sanctuary door), they synchronize admirably with the classical Renaissance ambience. If the figures are more stylized than realistic, producing anatomies somewhat reminiscent of El Greco's, it is because of Pickel's convic-

7.25 St. Anthony Mary Claret *and* St. Pius X *(Lower East Transept Windows)*

95

7.26 *The Dome.* Angels

7.28 *The Sacristy.* The Immaculate Conception

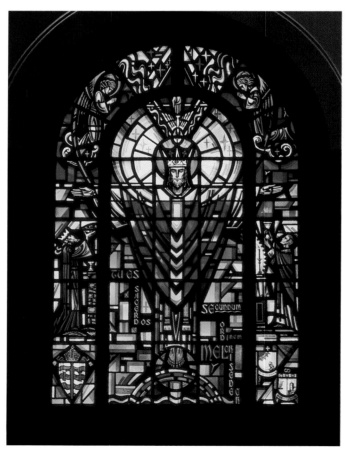

7.27 *The Sacristy.* Christ the High Priest

tion that "[a]...photographic likeness...would destroy the feeling that religion is timeless, sacred, apart from and above material things, and eternal in value."[10] A traditional touch, however, is provided by the Latin inscriptions. These include an excerpt from the rite of ordination — "You are a priest forever, according to the order of Melchizedek" (Psalm 110:4) — and the episcopal and familial mottoes of Archbishop Brady ("Justice, Peace, Joy," and "Love and Faithfulness," respectively).

The Paintings

Enhancing the inspirational as well as aesthetic appeal of the Cathedral's windows are paintings and sculpture displaying a mastery of design and deftness of touch equal to those of the glassmakers. Three large canvases, depicting events from the suffering and death of Christ, were hung soon after the opening of the edifice in 1915. On the north wall of the sanctuary, directly opposite the episcopal chair, is *The Entombment* (fig. 7.29) by Théodule-Augustin Ribot (1823-1891). Donated in 1919 by Mrs.

7.29 Théodule-Augustin Ribot, **The Entombment,** *undated.* Oil on canvas, 84⅝ x 58⅛₆ in. (215 x 147 cm)

James J. Hill, in whose husband's celebrated collection of nineteenth-century French art it once held a prominent place,[11] it is a dark and forbidding scene. Its darkness was inspired not so much by the tragedy of the episode, as by Ribot's deep respect for such seventeenth-century practitioners of "dark" realism as Jusepe de Ribera.[12] In contrast, the two works on the walls of the eastern piers display greater luminosity, though riven with the same sense of overwhelming sorrow pervading Ribot's treatment. To the south is the *Crucifixion* (fig. 7.30) by Nicholas Richard Brewer (1857-1949). Born near High Forest, Minnesota, and a long-time resident of St. Paul, Brewer became famous for his portraits especially of Henry Ward Beecher, Franklin Delano Roosevelt, and Archbishop Ireland. His rendition of Christ's death shows the sophistication of a mature artist; the muted tones convey deep suffering, but without distressing the viewer.[13] To the north is found *The Descent from the Cross* (fig. 7.31) by Karl-Ernest-Rodolphe-Heinrich-Salem Lehmann (1814-1882); it served as the altarpiece in the third Cathedral. Born in Germany, Lehmann studied in Paris under the greatest of all nineteenth-century classicists, Jean-Auguste-Dominique Ingres. The aesthetic creed of the master can be viewed in every aspect of this painting: the precision of line; the monumental forms, idealized and serene; and the evocation of a grand moment in time.[14]

The Four Evangelists

Monumental and elegant, too, is the most prominent sculptural ensemble in the Cathedral — that of the Four Evangelists set into the niches of the piers (figs. 7.32, 7.33, 7.34, 7.35). (This placement was not coincidental, according to Msgr. Lawrence Ryan, for as the piers hold up the church of stone, so the Word recorded by Matthew, Mark, Luke, and John sustains that Church not made by human hands.[15]) Designed by John Angel (1881-1960) of Sandy Hook, Connecticut, the statues, sculpted of Mankato creamstone, are enormous: each rises to a height of 11′6″ and weighs eight tons. Work on the figures began in the late 1950s. Tragically, Angel did not live to see either the completion or the installation of his work. At the time of his death in October 1960, only the representations of Mark and Luke, carved by Piccirilli of Pietrasanta, Italy, had been finished; those of Matthew and John were fashioned by Egisto Bertozzi, working from Angel's original models. On the day of its installation the statue of the "Beloved Disciple" was dedicated to the memory of Archbishop Murray, who had died five years earlier.

7.30 *Nicholas Richard Brewer,* Crucifixion, *undated.* Oil on canvas, 135¼ x 91¼ in. (344 x 233 cm)

7.31 Karl-Ernest-Rodolphe-Heinrich-Salem Lehmann, The Descent from the Cross, *1867.* Oil on canvas, 135 x 91⅛ in. (343 x 229 cm)

7.32 St. Mark (Southeastern Pier)

7.33 St. Matthew (Southwestern Pier)

7.34 St. John (Northwestern Pier)

Practical Concerns

In retrospect, it is no exaggeration to say that the interior of the Cathedral of St. Paul presents one of the most distinguished examples of twentieth-century American ecclesiastical decoration. Such a statement is a tribute to a large group of talented artists and craftsmen. But an equal amount of acclaim belongs to those Archbishops and rectors who selected men of so high a creative caliber. The embellishment of the Cathedral proceeded along the lines established by Archbishop Ireland and Masqueray. As in the beginning, the clergy continued to provide the spiritual stimulus and direction, while the laity contributed the artistic expertise and skill. Yet not all the skill expended by laymen upon the edifice was expressed in stained glass, or oil, or stone. Simultaneous with the embellishment of the windows and walls were the design and installation of heating, lighting, and sound systems. Under the floor or around the interior cornice worked engineers, assembling the means by which a suitable physical atmosphere for prayer would be assured.

A Proper Heating System

Given Minnesota's harsh climate through a substantial

7.35 St. Luke *(Northeastern Pier)*

part of the year, and because of the enormous size of the structure, heating was an early and major concern of the Executive Building Committee. At first the Committee considered buying heat from the St. Paul Public Service Heating Plant but the cost was prohibitive. At a meeting in January 1907, the group studied a proposal to locate a heating plant in the crypt.[16] However, the final plan, adopted some six years later, called for a separate power-house, to be built at the rear of the Cathedral, on the southern side of the old Berkey property.[17] After studying the methods by which the larger Canadian churches were heated, the Committee accepted the scheme of the Toltz Engineering Company of St. Paul.[18] Boilers would pro-duce between sixty and seventy pounds of pressure, to provide sufficient steam radiation. The heated air would be driven by three large fans, located under the sanctuary, through a complex system of ducts, and emitted from registers placed under each pew.[19]

The Problems of Lighting

If the challenge of heating such an expanse was met with relative ease, that of lighting it posed continuous and serious problems. The dimensions of the area requiring proper illumination were staggering. Was it truly possible to successfully light the entire 7,150 square feet beneath the dome from a ceiling one hundred and eight-six feet high? Masqueray's original system of indirect, cove light-ing above the cornice was ahead of its time, but proved impractical for daily use. Its upkeep was simply too difficult.[20] During the 1920s Maginnis and Walsh posi-tioned a series of large candelabras on the piers and the walls of the sanctuary, but they did little to increase the amount of light beyond their surrounding area. In exas-peration, Msgr. Lawrence Ryan suspended a seven-hundred-and-fifty-watt bulb from the center of the dome.

It was effective, if unsightly. In 1947, the present eight-pointed chandelier was installed.[21] Five years later, during the refurbishing of the interior of the dome, a new lighting scheme was introduced. It included pendants in the transepts, executed in the same neo-Gothic spirit of the chandelier, and floodlights in the dome and ceiling. To make this system even more effective, a major revamping was undertaken in 1976-1977, as part of the redecoration of the interior (fig. 7.36).

Sound and Music

Though as formidable as the problem of lighting, that of sound was resolved much more quickly and decisively. Critics who complained that the liturgy could not be heard, were silenced by the introduction of an effective public address system in October 1931. Closely related to this development were the efforts undertaken to assure that worship would be given a suitable musical accom-paniment. Brought over from the third Cathedral in 1915, the first organ in the new structure was used regularly until 1927, when a three manual, thirty rank Ernest Skinner model took its place in the sanctuary. Three decades later, Msgr. George Ryan authorized the Aeolian-Skinner Company of Boston to construct a second instru-ment, to be located in the choir loft. He insisted, however, that the new organ be playable from the existing sanctuary console, and vice-versa. Tonal synchronization of the two models required the rebuilding and revoicing of some of the ranks of the older, a complex and delicate process initiated only after a careful reassessment of the building's acoustics and the length of the reverberation period. The result was a skillful and harmonious blend of Classic and Baroque, offering great tonal variety and wide dynamic range. Installation of the piece in the loft was begun during the rectorate of Bishop Gerald F. O'Keefe, and continued through the first six months of 1963. On June 30, the coronation day of Pope Paul VI, as well as the patronal feast of the cathedral, the "Monsignor George E. Ryan Memorial Organ" was formally blessed by Arch-bishop Leo Binz at a Pontifical High Mass. When com-bined, the two organs contained seventy-one ranks, eighty stops, sixty voices, and 4,560 pipes. Their breathtaking sound has made the Cathedral one of the most popular sites for concerts in the Twin Cities.

By interweaving the work of designers, craftsmen, and engineers over a period of three decades, the Cathe-dral of St. Paul combined beauty and practicality, provid-ing an atmosphere in which spiritual needs and physical comfort were both addressed. This blend was realized only after the expenditure of much time, talent, and money. Yet the result — a warm and inviting place of prayer — shows that it was well worth the price.

7.36 The Present System of Interior Lighting

Chapter Eight

Middle-Age: The Second Ryan Era and Beyond, 1945-1990

*Overleaf: The Commemoration of the Cathedral's Consecration, October 14, 1958,
carved into the Tinos marble of the Southeastern (lower Selby Avenue) Vestibule*

he abrupt end of Msgr. Lawrence Ryan's rectorate in 1940 did not mean that the animated and ingenious work within the Cathedral over the previous twenty-five years was also at an end. For although it is true that nothing of artistic consequence was done by the two wartime rectors — John J. Cullinan (1940-1942) and Francis J. Schenk (1942-1945) — that inactivity, due largely to the scarcity of materials, laborers, and funds, was turned around completely by Msgr. George E. Ryan, beginning in June 1945. Under his supervision over the next fifteen years, the interior was cobwebbed with scaffolding and filled with the sound of hammers and chisels. That tempo continued under Ryan's two successors, bringing the structure to a state of completion that Ireland and Masqueray, more than half a century earlier, could only dream of seeing.

Msgr. George E. Ryan

Like his predecessor of the same name, Msgr. Ryan devoted much of his life to the continuing embellishment of the Cathedral (fig. 8.1). Though born in Hazelwood, Minnesota, he had spent his youth in St. Paul, playing in the shadow of the majestic dome and forming an attachment which would grow stronger as the years passed.[1] To the position of rector Ryan brought a wealth of pastoral experience acquired in parishes throughout the Archdiocese. Equally important, however, were his personal qualities and talents. Affable and outgoing, he was never happier than when he was addressing a civic or religious group, regaling it with stories culled either from the Cathedral's past or from his own extensive travels. As a raconteur, he was much in demand throughout the Twin Cities, and rarely turned down an offer to address a meeting or luncheon. His contemporaries wondered how he found the time both to serve his parishioners and continue the decoration of their church.[2] Yet he carried out both responsibilities successfully. Older parishioners still recall the high regard in which he was held by his congregation, while the myriad of projects executed inside the Cathedral during the decade of the fifties is eloquent proof that his vigor was not confined exclusively to the spinning of anecdotes. Project followed project, in a seemingly endless stream of things to be done. Barely was one design undertaken, that another was begun.

Some of the fruits of this fast-paced era have been discussed previously: the windows by Connick's associates, Weston, and Pickel; the statues by Angel; the chandelier in the dome and pendants in the transepts; and the decision to build an organ in the gallery. All of these, and more, owed their existence not only to Ryan's enthusiasm, but also to his amazing fund-raising ability and his refined artistic sense. He was himself at the forefront of every financial campaign; nor did his involvement end with his willingness to solicit resources throughout the State. He worked closely with artists and craftsmen, offering them ideas gleaned from his own studies of ecclesiastical art in Europe, and especially in Rome. For example, while it is widely known that the chandelier in the dome owes much to Ryan's input, the fact that he also contributed much to the planning of the confessional windows, lies buried in his correspondence with Connick's associates, filed in the Cathedral Archives.

8.1 Monsignor George E. Ryan

Work on the Dome, Roof, and Ceiling

In any event, there could be no doubt that the first work to be undertaken by Ryan — the proper insulation of the dome and roof area — was absolutely necessary. Ever since its opening, the structure had been plagued each winter by condensation on the interior of the copper roof. In time, this accumulation of moisture began to drip onto the plaster ceiling, causing cracks and peeling. In 1948, the Isco Corporation of St. Paul was commissioned to install a one-inch-thick insulation mat over the entire forty-eight thousand square feet of the roof's interior. The project required four years, and was completed in June 1952. During the process engineers were brought in to inspect the steel trusses located between the copper roofing and the ceiling of the interior. They pronounced them structurally sound.

Having dealt with the problem of condensation, Ryan next turned to the decoration of the ceiling and dome. Immediately after the placement of the insulation

8.2 The Gilded Interior of the Dome

began the coloring and application of gold leaf, following designs provided by Joseph A. Capecchi of West St. Paul (fig. 8.2). Carrying the spirit of Pennell, Gibbs, and Quiring's sanctuary ceiling through the main body of the church, Capecchi divided his surface area into richly bordered geometric shapes of various sizes. Though neither Masqueray nor Maginnis and Walsh had envisaged a painted, much less a gilded, ceiling, the result was much

in keeping with the idea of a grand yet restrained interior. The ornateness of the ceiling was tempered by the simplicity of the Mankato stone walls, just as the gold leaf added greater vibrancy to the flood of colored light through the three rose windows. To verbalize the joyful vigor of the forms on the ceiling, the text of Psalm 150 was painted at the base of the dome: "Praise ye the Lord in His sanctuary. Praise Him for His mighty deeds. Praise Him

dows of the angelic choirs were installed, chandeliers were hung in the transepts, and four mosaics were set in the pendentives of the dome. Designed by Michelangelo Bedini and executed by the Vatican Studios, the mosaics feature four heroic angels, representatives of the cardinal virtues, standing against a background of Venetian gold. Prudence carries a mirror, reminding the viewer that it is by "looking back" into the past that one finds the wisdom needed to guide present and future actions. The serpent in his other hand recalls the Scriptural injunction, "You must be clever as serpents..." (Matthew 10:16). Girded with a sword, Justice displays the scales, the sign of equity (fig. 8.3). Fortitude is accompanied by breastplate, helmet, and shield; his oak staff is a symbol of the firmness with which Christians must confront the world's difficulties. Temperance pours a liquid (the right amount) from a larger to a smaller vessel (fig. 8.4). The lesson conveyed is one of moderation. Seen from seventy feet below, these creations do not reveal either their true size or their method of composition. Each is twenty-five feet high by fifteen feet wide, and consists of tens of thousands of brilliantly colored tiles. As the only example of their medium currently in the structure, they speak well for the

8.3 Pendentive of the Dome. **Justice**

for His sovereign majesty. Praise Him with timbrel and chorus. Praise Him with strings and organ. Let everything that breathes praise the Lord." The entire work was completed in June 1954, at a cost of $200,000.

The Mosaics of the Virtues

During the refurbishing, Ryan decided to take advantage of the $36,000 worth of scaffolding already in place by making further improvements: Weston's twenty-four win-

8.4 Pendentive of the Dome. Temperance

Except for the monumental figures of the four Evangelists, discussed in Chapter Seven, all of the creative additions were small in size and subdued in spirit. The permanent Stations of the Cross, designed by Capecchi, were installed in 1956 (fig. 8.5). Consisting of cast bronze medallions set in oak crosses, "they are," according to Ryan, "like notes borrowed from the theme established by the sanctuary grille."[4] During the process of modelling the Stations, Capecchi also produced the tympana over the vestibule doors of the transepts, and a pair of bronze plaques, affixed to the northwestern pier, commemorating Pacelli's visit of 1936 and the episcopacy of the recently deceased John Gregory Murray. Working at the same time as Capecchi was the local firm of Brioschi and

8.5 One of the Fourteen Stations of the Cross

twentieth-century state of an art used by the Church since its earliest days. Moreover, they blend in perfectly with the painting, gilding, and glasswork covering the upper reaches of the nave and transepts.

Finishing the Crypt

With work on the Cathedral's upper reaches successfully begun, Ryan turned his attention to its lower level. In 1952, he escorted the officers of the parish societies through the crypt, telling them of his plans to finish its sadly neglected north side. Despite some initial questions as to whether the footings would support the burden of added walls and furnishings,[3] the enterprise went ahead; the commission was awarded to Bettenburg, Townsend, Stolte, and Comb of St. Paul. In 1955, a large complex of rooms was officially opened, as part of the celebration in honor of the rector's twenty-five years of priestly service. Included in the complex were a large meeting room (the Hall of the Angels), library, historical museum, kitchen, and a series of smaller workrooms. The cost of the project was $100,000.

Completion of the Interior Decoration

While the largest and most expensive undertakings of the second Ryan era were directed toward such practical ends as better lighting, more effective musical accompaniment, a dry roof, and more space, much talent and money were also spent in completing the decoration of the interior.

Son, which created the ornamental stonework on the transept balustrades and on the wall under the choir loft. Other artistic touches of the Ryan era included the statues in the side niches of the two chapels of the nave (Sts. Anne and Joachim, in that of the Blessed Virgin Mary; the Infant of Prague and St. Pius X, in that of St. Joseph), and the tall Ming burial urns, once part of the Louis W. Hill, Sr., collection of Oriental art, and positioned on the pedestals flanking the inner side of the main door into the nave.

Archbishop Brady and the Consecration of the Cathedral

The climax of the Ryan years came not long before their end. On October 14, 1958, in a five-hour rite, Archbishop William O. Brady consecrated the Cathedral.[5] To qualify for consecration a church must meet certain canonical criteria: it must be durably constructed, monumental in character, and substantially complete. At the same time there must be absolute certainty that the building will never fall into other hands for "profane," that is, non-religious, purposes. Given the strictness of these qualifications, the solemn act is not often performed. When it is, the ritual raises a church to a higher level of prestige. Thus was the Cathedral of St. Paul formally recognized as an edifice of merit, enjoying a permanent religious character, and worthy of assuming its place among the premier houses of worship in the United States.

Three reminders of the ceremony, one hidden and the other two quite visible, remain in the Cathedral to this day. At the height of the ritual, and following the blessing of the exterior and interior walls, Archbishop Brady placed within the main altar a silver box containing relics of the true cross, the Apostles, St. Ignatius of Antioch (an ancient martyr), St. Maria Goretti (a modern martyr), and St. Pius X. Around the walls still hang Capecchi's twelve gilded bronze crosses, along with their candleholders (fig. 8.6). Symbols of the Apostles, they were individually anointed and incensed; in line with centuries- old procedure, their candles provided the sole source of light for the nave and transepts through the first stage of the consecration. Finally, on the wall of the southeastern (lower Selby Avenue) vestibule is inscribed the commemoration of the event:

8.6 Monsignor George E. Ryan with one of the twelve crosses commemorating the consecration of October 14, 1958

Ad Perpetuam Rei Memoriam

This Cathedral Church of Saint Paul, the third Cathedral since the founding of the Diocese in 1850, was built between 1906 and 1915 and dedicated by Archbishop John Ireland, the first Archbishop of this See. His successor, Archbishop Austin Dowling, added the sacristy to the church and embellished the sanctuary with bronze grilles, completing also the auxiliary chapels as Shrines of the Nations. The third Archbishop of Saint Paul, John Gregory Murray, directed the liturgical completion of the main altar and the extensive interior decorations, installation of stained glass windows and beautification of the structure outside the sanctuary. This final work was carried on by the Rt. Rev. Msgr. George E. Ryan, Rector, who presented the completed structure to the fourth Archbishop of Saint Paul, the Most Rev. Wm. O. Brady, for consecration. Solemn consecration of the high altar and this Cathedral church took place on October 14, 1958.

Although the consecration was Ryan's greatest triumph as rector, it was also his last, for he died unexpectedly some two years later, on December 26, 1960. His successor, Bishop Gerald F. O'Keefe, inherited a virtually complete structure. His six-year tenure was aimed primarily at upkeep. Yet his was the honor of hosting a singular episode in the annals of the Cathedral. On Sunday, October 7, 1962, only two weeks before the Cuban missile crisis, he welcomed John F. Kennedy to the eleven o'clock Mass (fig. 8.7). A small plaque marks the pew in which the President worshiped.

8.7 President John F. Kennedy arrives for eleven o'clock Mass at the Cathedral, October 7, 1962.
At the right stands Bishop Gerald F. O'Keefe

8.8 The Exterior Lighting System

110

Succeeding O'Keefe, who was appointed Bishop of Davenport, Iowa, in 1966, was Msgr. Ambrose V. Hayden, whose twenty-three year rectorate has produced a number of improvements, some born of necessity, and others of the desire to fulfill the intentions of the original builders. Strictly speaking, the first effort of the new administration was neither absolutely necessary nor part of the Irelandian scheme. Furthermore, its impetus came not from the Archdiocese or the Cathedral authorities, but from the St. Paul Area Chamber of Commerce, which offered to pay the total cost of installing an exterior lighting system. The organization justified its proposal by appealing to a mixture of spiritual and practical considerations: the nocturnal illumination not only would honor one of the State's great monuments of faith, but also would add to the beauty and safety of its surrounding area. Based on studies of lighting used at the U.S. Capitol, the Sioux Falls Cathedral — incidentally, another Masqueray creation — and the Westminster Presbyterian and Hennepin Avenue Methodist Churches in Minneapolis, the system for the Cathedral of St. Paul was installed in 1967 (fig. 8.8). The edifice was illuminated from all sides, with emphasis on the dome. Special care was taken to conceal all lights within the structure. The outlay was $55,000. As part of the agreement, Cathedral authorities would pay the cost of electricity and maintenance. The civic leaders' gesture of esteem was re-echoed on a wider scale in 1974, when the Cathedral was listed in the National Register of Historical Buildings.

Vandalism and Restoration

Yet the civic and national recognition of the Cathedral's special place in the history of its city, state, and country, did not prevent vandals from breaking into the building on December 5, 1974, and setting a number of fires in the crypt.[6] The fires were not the first in the building's history. About a month after the dedication in 1915, a pile of discarded construction material, placed near the wall at the corner of Summit and Selby Avenues, was accidentally set alight. Then, in 1932, a mentally disturbed teenager started fires in five different areas of the edifice.[7] But whereas the earlier misfortunes had caused only minor damage — two cracked blocks of granite as a result of the first and some blackened walls in the crypt, in the wake of the second — that of 1974 ravaged the parish library and damaged small areas of the Cana Chapel, sending enormous amounts of smoke and soot into the main body of the church. Though the building was reopened for worship only twenty-four hours after the fire, it was clear that a more permanent scar had been left within the nave and transepts, one which the Fire Department's huge fans

could not blow away along with the soot and smell. The long-term legacy of the still unknown arsonists was an enormous increase of dirt embedded in the stone, plasterwork, and glass of the dome, ceiling, and walls.

A complete cleaning and refurbishing of the interior was begun in August 1976, and completed in time for Holy Week, 1977 (fig. 8.9).[8] Carried out by a St. Paul Statuary Company crew, among whom were Joseph Capecchi's sons and grandsons, the project included, in addition to restoration work, repairs on the dome and upper levels of the nave, and the placement of a new lighting system by Rambusch and Company. Reflective lighting was installed along the cornice, while vapor lights were interspersed among the already existing floodlights in the dome. The entire enterprise amounted to $360,000. Through the eight-month process, the Cathedral continued to function normally; liturgies, including those of Christmas, were celebrated under "a maze of scaffolding and hundreds of feet of plastic..."[9] The financial cost and physical inconvenience, however, paled before the jewel-like brilliance of the resurrected interior. In its entirety it was nothing less than a feast for the eyes.

A New "Voice"

A spiritual appeal to the ears followed a decade later, with the installation and dedication of five new bells. The absence of a series of bells worthy of the edifice had become increasingly obvious over the years. Between 1915 and 1986 the Cathedral's "voice" consisted of one bell, cast in Cincinnati in 1850. It had been given to Bishop Cretin by Louis Robert, and had hung in the second and third cathedrals, before being installed in the south tower of the present Mother Church. In 1985, at the instigation of Msgr. Hayden, it was decided to install a new peal of five bells (fig. 8.10). Besides providing a sound as grand as the structure for which it was cast, the group possessed a sentimental significance: the Paccard foundry, its birthplace, was located in Annecy, France, a city not far from Montluel, Bishop Cretin's birthplace, and Meximieux, the site of John Ireland's days as a seminarian. Also nearby is the town of Ars, home of St. John Vianney, a secondary patron of the Archdiocese, who, as already seen, is honored in one of the windows of the south transept. The set was blessed by Archbishop John R. Roach at a special Mass of June 7, 1987 (fig. 8.11).

Following ancient custom, each of the bells is dedicated to one or more saints. For obvious reasons, the largest, weighing 6,600 pounds and pitched to "Bf2," bears the name of St. Paul; on it is inscribed the text of Romans 10:18, "Their voice has sounded over all the earth." Next in size is the bell of the Blessed Virgin Mary, weighing 4,630 pounds and pitched to "C3" (fig. 8.12). It

8.9 The Interior under Restoration, 1976-1977

112

8.10 The Five New Bells Stand in the Cathedral Parking Lot, Awaiting Installation

bears the opening phrase of the *Magnificat:* "My soul proclaims the greatness of the Lord" (Luke 1:46). The third largest bell carries a dedication to the three most celebrated members of that heavenly choir which gives constant praise and glory to God, the Archangels Michael, Gabriel, and Raphael. Its weight stands at 2,750 pounds, its pitch at "D3," and it bears the words, "Bless the Lord, O you his angels" (Psalm 103:20). To commemorate the advances of the American Church, the fourth bell is dedicated to St. Frances Xavier Cabrini. In recognition of her intense love for the poor and suffering, it features the words of Matthew 25:35, "I was a stranger and you welcomed me." The bell weighs 1,990 pounds and is pitched to "F3." The name of St. John Vianney is embossed on the smallest bell, weighing 1,545 pounds and pitched to "C3." Along with the name of the celebrated confessor visited by Ireland during his seminary days, is the expression of praise found in Psalm 108:5, "Your mercy, O Lord, is great above the heavens." Each of the five bells was cast of the finest bronze, consisting of 78% pure copper and 22% tin. Altogether, the casting, transportation, and installation (but not the preparation of the tower) amounted to $140,000.

Well into the fourth and fifth decades of its existence, the Cathedral continued to grow in important ways. Msgr. George E. Ryan accomplished what many thought they would never live to see: the completion of the interior. Combining his contributions to the edifice with those of his predecessor of the same name, it has been said that the name of Ryan stands second only to those of Ireland and Masqueray on a list of the Cathedral's benefactors.[10] Such a claim is not meant to overlook the achievements of more recent rectors, to whom fell the equally challenging responsibility of maintenance and refinement. For during the sixth and seventh decades of John Ireland's "great temple on the hill," the creations of earlier years have been revivified and enhanced, reminding Minnesotans in a dramatic new way of the eternal spiritual truths to which they bear witness.

8.11 John R. Roach, Seventh Archbishop of St. Paul and Minneapolis, after the Blessing of the Bells, June 7, 1987

113

8.12 The Installation of the Bell Dedicated to the Blessed Virgin, December 16, 1986

Conclusion

The Cathedral of Saint Paul as Structure and Symbol

Overleaf: *The Paschal Candlestick.* This extraordinary example of Florentine neo-Renaissance craftsmanship was brought to St. Paul by Joseph A. Capecchi, and donated to the Cathedral by Amerigo Brioschi and Adelmo Rossi.

As it approaches the seventy-fifth anniversary of its dedication, the Cathedral of Saint Paul continues to be the subject of ongoing proposals for the embellishment of its few incomplete areas. The two pedestals flanking the front steps await the over life-size renditions of Father Galtier and Archbishop Ireland, the former turned toward the river which served as the conduit for his missionary activity, and the latter facing the State Capitol across the expansive thoroughfare named in his honor.[1] Preliminary designs for the statues indicate that their heroic quality is in keeping with the Michelangelesque sculpture of the facade. At the same time, these figures complete the message carved within and on the borders of the monumental arch, by showing how Christ's commission, carried out first by the Apostles, was then taken up, albeit on a smaller stage, by the first priest and the first Archbishop of St. Paul. It may be added that the choice of Galtier and Ireland for such an honor is singularly appropriate, given the fact that neither has been given a remembrance of any significance within the structure.

In a similar vein, the various suggestions for additions to the interior involve recognition of distinguished service to the Church. Within the east wall of each transept rests an empty eleven-by-eighteen-foot panel, to be filled eventually by a canvas. That on the north (Dayton Avenue) side will feature Bishop Cretin's arrival in St. Paul; greeting the purple-robed prelate at the dock will be Father Ravoux, along with a few settlers and native Americans. In the background, atop the bluff, will stand Galtier's log chapel, the first Cathedral of St. Paul. A sharp contrast to this scene of simple faith in the wilderness, the painting on the south (Selby Avenue) side will re-create the dedication of the present Mother Church; a splendidly bedecked Archbishop Ireland, his hand extended in blessing, will lead his people in procession around the edifice.[2] The grandeur of the building and the ceremony surrounding it point to the breathtaking strides made by Minnesota Catholicism over a period of only sixty years.

Often mentioned is the possibility of placing statues of Saints Ambrose and Augustine upon the empty pedestals positioned against the wall under the choir gallery. (Until a few years ago, the pedestals held the Ming vases introduced by Msgr. George Ryan.) However, the question of whether or not to place anything at all upon the pedestals, has yet to be resolved. Far more certain of eventual placement are two notable additions to the narthex. Affixed to the north wall of the Founders' Chapel will be a plaque commemorating John Ireland's role as cathedral-builder. In the west wall of the baptistry will be set a mosaic of the Baptism of Christ by John. Designs for each of these are currently being prepared, in the hope that their installation will be finished in time for the observance of the diamond jubilee.

After more than seven decades of service, and long after virtually all of its designers and craftsmen have died, the Cathedral of Saint Paul continues to grow and change. The aforementioned proposals are eloquent proof that Ireland's temple on the hill is not a static, ossified landmark; on the contrary, this *grande dame* of a metropolis named after her, continues to capture the affection of new generations of churchmen and artists, eager to expend upon her the same levels of creativity and energy as had their predecessors.

Yet, in the long run, the Cathedral of Saint Paul is more than a product of artistic talent and clerical drive. To see the structure exclusively in architectural terms, that is, as a skillful arrangement of stone, metal, wood, and glass costing a total of $1,600,000, is to minimize its role in the continuing development of its people, city, and state. More than a historical curiosity, or an artistic wonder, or a theological statement, it is a multi-faceted symbol, proffering an array of rich meanings. This being the case, well might John Henry Newman's definition of a Cathedral as "a sort of world," apply to the Irelandian edifice.[3]

At its simplest level, the Cathedral is a personal symbol, enjoying a distinct place in the life of each of its familiars. Those inquiring into the building's history will quickly discover that almost everyone in the Twin Cities possesses at least one unique and treasured memory of it, whether joyful or sad. The importance of the Cathedral as a private symbol cannot be overestimated. The emphasis in this narrative upon the Archbishops, rectors, artists, and craftsmen should not obscure the central fact that Ireland's and Masqueray's vision was realized only through the sacrifices of thousands of individuals. In addition to financial donations, ranging from one schoolgirl's offering of five cents to William C. Riley's endowment of almost half a million dollars, many offered their labor. So zealous in their work were the paid construction teams that Ireland visited them often, as a sign of his great affection and respect. During one such visit, shortly before the completion of the interior, the Archbishop was introduced to one of the men involved in the installation of the pews. The worker hesitated to extend his hand, indicating that it was covered with linseed oil and putty; Ireland responded, "If you can wash your hands, I can wash mine," and took his hand.[4] Motivated by a similar spirit of respect, Msgr. Lawrence Ryan, who had watched the Cathedral rise above its hill, repeatedly paid homage to "the brawn, artistry and sweat of many a begrimed worker...imbedded in...[the]...walls and piers."[5] With their dedication and selflessness as credentials, thousands of donors and workers had every right to point to the completed edifice, as did the flamboyant stonemason, Nils Nelson, and call it, "My building."

In an equally valid sense, however, "My building" is also "Our building," for the house of worship which shelters so many precious memories and hopes, is at the same time a parish church. Like any of the other two hundred and nineteen parishes in the Archdiocese of St. Paul and Minneapolis, the Cathedral building is the center of a functioning community of believers. Over the years

thousands of Masses, baptisms, confirmations, marriages, and funerals have been celebrated for the Catholics of the surrounding residential area. Although the number of parishioners has declined since the mid-1960s, due to the disappearance of a substantial portion of nearby homes, in the wake of freeway construction and commercial development, the parish remains a day-to-day spiritual home for many.

On a larger scale, the Cathedral of Saint Paul can justifiably claim a unique and continuing place in the development of its city and state. The central role of its three predecessors in the life of a growing pioneer town already has been outlined; the fourth Mother Church

Church and State in the City of St. Paul. Referring to the artistic harmony between Masqueray's Cathedral and his own design for the State Capitol, Cass Gilbert, the internationally famous architect, contended that "if the dome of the Cathedral of St. Paul and that of the new State Capitol were part of the skyline of a city in Europe, they would be world famous."

enjoys a significance no less formidable. On the one hand, it is for many non-Catholics as well as Catholics, the prime religious edifice of the Twin Cities: what resident of Minneapolis or St. Paul has been able to resist the temptation to show it off to visiting family and friends? While its majestic location and architectural grandeur certainly account for much of the local pride it engenders, they do not account for all of it. Beyond these rather obvious determinants is yet another: the Cathedral is an ongoing sign of the faith and idealism of the men and women who first settled the Twin Cities. Viewed in this light, another astounding fact becomes understandable: in a period of history not known for its ecumenism, not only did Protestants enthusiastically join with Catholics to celebrate the laying of the cornerstone, but "businessmen of all faiths" sat on the committee entrusted with the task of raising the funds for the construction of the dome.[6] Moreover, the Cathedral's status as the preeminent ecclesiastical structure of its area has earned it a place as one of the points of that triangle of key human activities plotted within downtown St. Paul. Balancing the spiritual accomplishments of humanity, as represented by Ireland's church, are the political, symbolized by the equally impressive State Capitol, and the commercial, for which the skyscrapers serve as the emblem.[6]

On the other hand, there is an equally important non-religious role played by the Cathedral. Not only does it form a breathtaking crown for the brow of St. Anthony Hill; it serves as a fitting introduction to Summit Avenue, St. Paul's premier thoroughfare, and the location of two other Irelandian legacies, the College of St. Thomas and the St. Paul Seminary. From the latter, situated at the other end of the majestic corridor, come the young men who, in the shadow of Warren's baldachin, receive the ministry of Christ Himself. Of course, for the overwhelming majority of Minnesotans, contact with the Cathedral does not involve so dramatic a change of life. Concert-goers repeatedly fill its pews. Its acoustical qualities, though challenging because of the lengthy reverberation time, make it a place in which many local and visiting classical musicians enjoy performing. Marathon-runners stride past its facade each October, while children, almost every afternoon, scamper up its front steps or maneuver precariously along the ground-level ledges of the transepts. Rarely is the edifice empty of camera-laden tourists, who come from every part of the world. Of different backgrounds, faiths, and languages, they share the same experience as they pass through its doors: the almost instinctive and irresistible urge to look up into the dome; and from that "[symphony] of space so architecturally perfect that size is merely an illusion," their eyes sweep slowly across the

great arches of the nave and transepts, ultimately coming to rest in the sanctuary, at the main altar.[7]

As the Cathedral of Saint Paul celebrates its diamond jubilee, its major place in both the history of Minnesota Catholicism and the development of American ecclesiastical architecture is secure. Yet, its variety of treasures notwithstanding, it is more than a museum-piece. It is a living, growing symbol of humanity's effort to become one with the Divine. It is a joyous affirmation of that faith which Edmund Bishop, the renowned English liturgist, called "the everlasting yea."[8] It is the visible heart of the Church in Minnesota, expressing the hopes and inspiring the prayers of generations to come, just as it has done over the past three-quarters of a century.

Overleaf: Christmas at the Cathedral of Saint Paul

NOTES, APPENDICES
& BIBLIOGRAPHY

NOTES

The following abbreviations have been used throughout in the citation of sources:

ACHS Archives of the Catholic History Society of St. Paul

ACSP Archives of the Cathedral of Saint Paul

Chapter One

1 "The New Cathedral," *The New Cathedral Bulletin* 1 (August 1904): 1.

2 *Northwestern Chronicle,* 10 May 1889.

3 Cited in Robert Gray, *Cardinal Manning; A Biography* (London: Weidenfeld and Nicolson, 1985), 206-7. On Ireland's admiration for the Archbishop of Westminster, see James H. Moynihan, *The Life of Archbishop John Ireland* (New York: Harper & Brothers, 1953), 320-1.

4 "Meeting of the Board of Consultors (Address of the Archbishop)," *The New Cathedral Bulletin* 1 (August 1904): 11.

5 There are two full-length biographies of John Ireland. The first (Moynihan, *op. cit.*) has recently been superseded by that of Marvin R. O'Connell, *John Ireland and the American Catholic Church* (St. Paul: Minnesota Historical Society Press, 1988).

6 Archbishop John Ireland, *The Church and Modern Society; Lectures and Addresses* (St. Paul: The Pioneer Press, 1904-5), I, 119-20.

7 *Ibid.,* 89.

8 *Ibid.,* 74.

9 *Ibid.,* 115.

10 "Archbishop Keane's Sermon (Funeral of Archbishop Ireland, 2 October 1918)," in *Archbishop Ireland: Prelate-Patriot-Publicist, 1838-1918; A Memoir,* ed. James M. Reardon (St. Paul: The Catholic Bulletin, n.d.), 28.

11 Cited in Shane Leslie, *Cardinal Gasquet; A Memoir* (London: Burns Oates, 1953), 34.

12 "Archbishop Keane's Sermon (Funeral of Archbishop Ireland, 2 October 1918)," in *Archbishop Ireland: Prelate-Patriot-Publicist, 1838-1918; A Memoir,* 28.

13 Ireland, *op. cit.,* viii-ix.

14 *The New Cathedral of St. Paul; Letter of the Most Reverend Archbishop* (St. Paul: Privately printed, 1905), n.p.

15 *Acta et Dicta* 3 (July 1914): 324.

16 For a list of Masqueray's major ecclesiastical commissions in the Midwest, see Appendix Two, p. 128.

17 *Catholic Bulletin,* 9 June 1917. For a detailed appreciation of Masqueray's life and multi-faceted career, see Alan K. Lathrop, "A French Architect in Minnesota: Emmanuel L. Masqueray, 1861-1917," *Minnesota History* 46 (Summer 1980): 42-56.

18 *Ibid.,* 46.

19 *Acta et Dicta* 3 (July 1914): 324.

20 *Catholic Bulletin,* 29 July 1911.

21 *Catholic Bulletin,* 17 October 1958.

Chapter Two

1 Cited in A. McNulty, "The Chapel of St. Paul, The Cradle of the Catholic Church in Minnesota," *Acta et Dicta* 1 (July 1907): 66.

2 Galtier to Bishop Grace, 14 January 1864, cited in *ibid.,* 65.

3 *Ibid.,* 67-8.

4 *Ibid.,* 68-9.

5 For the fate of the abandoned and later dismantled log chapel-cathedral, see *ibid.,* 71-2.

6 For a detailed description of the three floors, accompanied by diagrams, see Anatole Oster, "Personal Reminiscences of Bishop Cretin," *Acta et Dicta* 1 (July 1907): 74-6.

7 *Ibid.,* 74-5.

8 Archbishop John Ireland, "Sermon Presented at the Final Service of the Old Cathedral of St. Paul," *Acta et Dicta* 4 (July 1915): 82.

9 *Ibid.,* 83.

10 Ireland, *op. cit.,* 85.

11 *Ibid.*

12 "Personal Reminiscences of Mr. Wharton Smith, March 1973" (ACSP).

Chapter Three

1 *Northwestern Chronicle,* 21 July 1887.

2 *Midway News,* 1 March 1890.

3 *Midway News,* 29 June 1889.

4 *Northwestern Chronicle,* 21 July 1887.

5 *Supra,* 14.

6 "Personal Reminiscences of Charles H.F. Smith (Undated)" (ACSP).

7 *Ibid.*

8 Smith to Ireland, 14 April 1904 (ACSP). Interestingly, Smith purchased the property in his own name, so as not to betray the Archbishop's intentions to the owners, St. Paul Title and Trust Company and Almeric H. Paget. Upon receiving the deed, Smith transferred it to Ireland ("Personal Reminiscences of Mr. Wharton Smith, March 1973" [ACSP]).

9 "Personal Reminiscences of Charles H.F. Smith (Undated)." Smith, who later headed the Executive Building Committee for the New Cathedral, concludes that if up to that time Ireland had entertained any doubts about the worthiness of the project, they were completely dispelled by this meeting: "...he accepted the task, feeling that God would help him to accomplish what would be a testimonial to his faith in the Almighty Who Knows All."

10 "The New Cathedral," *The New Cathedral Bulletin* 1 (August 1904): 5. For a sample of the enthusiasm of non-Catholics as well as Catholics for the Cathedral project in general, see *ibid.,* 3-8.

11 *Ibid.,* 2.

12 *Ibid.,* 8. The specific role of the Board, according to Ireland, was to "take charge of all contributions to the project, keep informed on all matters pertaining to the work, hear reports from special committees, give suggestions and awaken a general interest throughout the city" (*ibid.,* 10).

13 Ireland to Smith, 20 July 1904 (ACSP).

14 Ireland to Smith, 23 July 1904 (ACSP).

15 For details of the meeting at Raudenbush Hall, see "The New Cathedral," 10-12. The members of the Board are listed in *ibid.,* 9-10.

16 The original members of the Committee were Ireland, Father Patrick R. Heffron, Father John J. Lawler, Father Thomas J. Gibbons, Father Ambrose McNulty, Father John M. Solnce, Charles H.F. Smith, Louis W. Hill, H.C. McNair, Judge Edward W. Bazille, John S. Grode, Timothy Foley, Christopher D. O'Brien, Jeremiah C. Kennedy, Constantine J. McConville, George N. Gerlach, Thomas Fitzpatrick, and John B. Meagher. Others were added to fill vacancies caused by death or resignation: Father F.X. Bajec, Father F.X. Gores, Peter M. Kerst, Francis M. Erling, George Michel, J.C. Nolan, Charles Friend, Jr., Frank Schlick, and H. Von der Weyer ("Minutes of the Meetings of the Executive Building Committee of the New Cathedral" [ACSP]).

17 *Ibid.*

18 *St. Paul Pioneer Press,* 29 January 1905.

19 Their letters of acceptance, some of which are lengthy due to the inclusion of several reservations, are found in the Ireland papers (ACHS).

20 Brown to Ireland, 11 March 1905, in *ibid.*

21 Fitzpatrick to O'Brien, 6 February 1905, cited in Alan K. Lathrop, "A French Architect in Minnesota: Emmanuel L. Masqueray, 1861-1917," *Minnesota History* 46 (Summer 1980): 44.

22 Masqueray to Ireland, 23 March 1905 (ACHS).

23 McGuire to O'Brien, 23 March 1905 (*ibid.*).

24 Carrère and Hastings to O'Brien, 23 March 1905 (*ibid*).

25 *Ibid.*

26 Fitzpatrick to O'Brien, 6 February 1905 (*ibid.*).

27 See the letter from Masqueray to O'Brien, 6 February 1905, in *ibid.*

28 Fuzet to Ireland, 3 August 1905 (*ibid.*).

29 For the most complete explanation of the original design by the architect himself, see E.L. Masqueray, "Religious Architecture and the Cathedral of St. Paul and Pro-Cathedral of the Immaculate Conception," *Western Architect* 12 (October 1908): 43-4.

30 Lathrop, *op. cit.,* 50. Coincidentally, it was Masqueray's first instructor at the Ecole des Beaux-Arts, Charles-Jean Laisné, who was in charge of the construction of Sacré-Coeur from 1886 to 1891.

31 Masqueray, *op. cit.,* 43.

32 *Supra,* 8; Masqueray, *op. cit.,* 44.

33 *The New Cathedral of St. Paul; Letter of the Most Reverend Archbishop* (St. Paul: Privately Printed, 1905), n.p.

34 Entry of 8 October 1904, in "Minutes of the Meetings of the Executive Building Committee of the New Cathedral."

35 Entry of 15 November 1905, in *ibid.*

36 Over fifty years later, Msgr. George E. Ryan recalled, "...my brothers and sisters and I each had round nickelplated banks with a name-plate on them, 'For the New Cathedral.' In them we saved our coins and when they were full we would take them to our pastor to be opened and emptied so we could continue our good work" (*Catholic Bulletin,* 17 October 1958). For Ireland's letter to one child who pledged her savings, see Marvin R. O'Connell, *John Ireland and the American Catholic Church* (St. Paul: Minnesota Historical Society Press, 1988), 502.

37 *The New Cathedral of St. Paul; Letter of the Most Reverend Archbishop,* n.p. See also O'Connell, *loc. cit.*

38 Advertisement sponsored by the Committee on Subscriptions for the New Cathedral, undated (ACSP).

Chapter Four

1 James M. Reardon, *The Catholic Church in the Diocese of St. Paul from Earliest Origins to Centennial Achievement* (St. Paul: North Central Publishing Company, 1952), 375-6.

2 Entry of 14 November 1906, in "Minutes of the Meetings of the Executive Building Committee of the New Cathedral" (ACSP). The Archdiocese made another attempt to buy the property in mid-1910. Berkey was prepared to lower his asking price to $65,000, but the Committee now decided that it would pay no more than $30,000, which it deemed the true value of the sixty-foot-wide parcel (entry of 3 June 1910, in *ibid.*). The land was finally acquired in October 1913, for $35,000, to be used as the site of the Cathedral's heating plant (entry of 3 October 1913, in *ibid.*).

3 *Northwestern Chronicle,* 11 August 1906; *St. Paul Pioneer Press,* 25 October 1906. The land ceded by the Archdiocese included sixty-four feet along the east side of Summit Avenue and eighty-nine feet on Dayton Avenue. The original estimate of replacing water mains and repaving was approximately $11,000 (entry of 14 November 1906, in "Minutes of the Meetings of the Executive Building Committee of the New Cathedral"); two months later it was raised to $15,900 (entry of 11

January 1907, in *ibid.*). In the long run, the city did not move the water mains; they remain to this day submerged under the main stairway of the Cathedral.

4 Entry of 5 July 1906, in *ibid..*

5 Marvin R. O'Connell, *John Ireland and the American Catholic Church* (St. Paul: Minnesota Historical Society Press, 1988), 504.

6 Entry of 11 January 1907, in "Minutes of the Meetings of the Executive Building Committee of the New Cathedral."

7 *Ibid.*

8 Entry of 5 July 1906, in *ibid.*

9 The seven firms were George J. Grant, Newman & Hoy, Lauer Brothers, J.M. Carlson, P.M. Hennessy Construction Company, Butler Brothers, and T. Reardon (entry of 16 August 1906, in *ibid.*).

10 *Ibid.* The original bid would be increased $958 by mid-November, due to Masqueray's changes in designs.

11 Masqueray to the Executive Building Committee, 22 October 1906 (ACSP).

12 Entry of 26 February 1907, in "Minutes of the Meetings of the Executive Building Committee of the New Cathedral."

13 Entries of 11 January and 14 February 1907, in *ibid.*

14 Entry of 14 May 1907, in *ibid.*

15 Entries of 24 October and 14 November 1906, in *ibid.*

16 For a detailed description of the ceremony, see "The Laying of the Corner Stone of The New Cathedral," *Acta et Dicta* 1 (July 1907): 99-151. An informal view of the proceedings is provided by Msgr. Lawrence F. Ryan, "Historical Sketch of the Cathedral of St. Paul, 1904-1937" (ACSP).

17 *St. Paul Pioneer Press,* 3 June 1907.

18 *Ibid.,* 1 June 1907; "The Laying of the Corner Stone of The New Cathedral," 110-1.

19 *Ibid.,* 113-5. The full text of the parchment, in English translation, is in *ibid.,* 146-51.

20 *Ibid.,* 115.

21 *Ibid.*

22 Ryan, *op. cit.*

23 "The Laying of the Corner Stone of The New Cathedral," 118.

24 *Northwestern Chronicle,* 14 May 1904.

25 Smith to Ireland, 9 December 1908 (ACSP).

26 Ireland to Smith, 27 December 1908 (ACSP).

27 Entry of 21 January 1908, in "Minutes of the Meetings of the Executive Building Committee of the New Cathedral." Ireland's fullest explanation of the rationale behind the additional assessment is found in his letter to the pastors of the Archdiocese, 20 May 1911 (ACHS).

28 Entry of 21 April 1908, in "Minutes of the Meetings of the Executive Building Committee of the New Cathedral."

29 Entry of 2 August 1909, in *ibid.*

30 Entry of 17 September 1909, in *ibid.* Ireland's own justification for the selection of granite was given in July 1912, during the ceremony commemorating the erection of the cross over the facade:

> The material used in the building — what better does America provide? It is granite, to forebode the enduring strength of the Cathedral and of its message to humanity — granite from Minnesota's own rich bosom, to proclaim Minnesota's own sufficiency to dare and to do the best — granite, lucid and sparkling, soft and living, as Minnesota's own skies and landscapes (*Acta et Dicta* 3 [July 1914]: 323).

31 Entry of 3 June 1910, in "Minutes of the Meetings of the Executive Building Committee of the New Cathedral."

32 *St. Paul Dispatch,* 20 September 1910. As the massive stone, still known today as the "Vannutelli lintel," was put in place above the door, the Cardinal applauded enthusiastically, while Ireland shouted out to Nils Nelson, one of P.M. Hennessy's best stoneworkers and the man in charge of the placement, "First class, Nelson!"

33 Entry of 18 July 1910, in "Minutes of the Meetings of the Executive Building Committee of the New Cathedral."

34 Quoted from an advertisement for the lecture (ACSP).

35 *Acta et Dicta* 3 (July 1914): 325.

36 Entry of 24 August 1912, in "Minutes of the Meetings of the Executive Building Committee of the New Cathedral."

37 John B. McCormack to an unidentified recipient, 19 September 1912; Lawrence A. Carr to Thomas F. McMahon, 3 May 1977 (ACSP).

38 *Acta et Dicta* 3 (July 1914): 326-7; Ryan, *op. cit.*

39 *Acta et Dicta* 3 (July 1914): 327-9.

40 Ryan, *op. cit.*

41 Entry of 21 October 1910, in "Minutes of the Meetings of the Executive Building Committee of the New Cathedral."

42 Msgr. George E. Ryan, cited in the *Catholic Bulletin,* 17 October 1958.

43 On the sculpture of the facade, see the *Catholic Bulletin,* 24 February 1912 and 10 April 1915.

Chapter Five

1 Msgr. Lawrence F. Ryan, "Historical Sketch of the Cathedral of St. Paul, 1904-1937" (ACSP).

2 Entry of 23 March 1914, in "Minutes of the Meetings of the Executive Building Committee of the New Cathedral" (ACSP).

3 Entry of 31 March 1914, in *ibid.*

4 Ryan, "Historical Sketch of the Cathedral of St. Paul, 1904-1937."

5 For details of this ceremony, see "Final Services in the Old Cathedral of Saint Paul," *Acta et Dicta* 4 (July 1915): 77-99.

6 *Ibid.,* 91-2.

7 *Ibid.,* 93.

8 Ryan, "Historical Sketch of the Cathedral of St. Paul, 1904-1937," and "Sermon Preached on the Occasion of the Fiftieth Anniversary of the Opening of the New Cathedral" (ACSP). Another eyewitness, John McCormack, one of the owners of the Rockville quarry, noted that "[as] the Archbishop said Mass, ...he looked ten years younger" (letter to an unidentified recipient, 29 March 1915 [ACSP]).

9 "Final Services in the Old Cathedral of Saint Paul," 105.

10 Ryan, "Historical Sketch of the Cathedral of St. Paul, 1904-1937."

11 "Final Services in the Old Cathedral of Saint Paul," 109-17.

12 Letter of 14 March 1915, cited in *ibid.,* 119.

13 Gasparri to Ireland, 19 March 1915, and Falconio to Ireland, 14 March 1915, cited in *ibid.,* 120-1.

14 Ryan, "Historical Sketch of the Cathedral of St. Paul, 1904-1937."

15 For a detailed description of the chapel, see the *Catholic Bulletin,* 13 November 1915 and 17 April 1920.

16 Ryan, "Historical Sketch of the Cathedral of St. Paul, 1904-1937."

17 *Catholic Bulletin,* 17 January 1914 and 12 February 1916.

18 James L. Esser, "The Cathedral of Saint Paul, St. Paul, Minnesota: An Architectural, Historical, and Descriptive Narrative" (Unpublished research paper, University of Minnesota, 1966), 33.

19 Louis M. Hastings to André Delamare, 21 June 1917 (ACHS).

20 Keane to Ireland, 26 May 1917, cited in the *Catholic Bulletin,* 2 June 1917.

21 *Catholic Bulletin,* 9 June 1917.

22 Ryan, "Historical Sketch of the Cathedral of St. Paul, 1904-1937."

23 *Ibid.*

24 *Ibid.*

25 Marvin R. O'Connell, *John Ireland and the American Catholic Church* (St. Paul: Minnesota Historical Society Press, 1988), 516.

Chapter Six

1 For a synopsis of Archbishop Dowling's life, work, and character, see Marvin R. O'Connell, "Archdiocese of Saint Paul," in *Catholic Heritage in Minnesota, North Dakota, and South Dakota,* ed. Patrick H. Ahern (St. Paul: The Province of St. Paul, 1964), 33-5.

2 In May, John J. Lawler, the first rector of the new Cathedral, was installed as Bishop of Lead, South Dakota. His successor, Thomas J. Gibbons, formerly of St. Luke's Church (St. Paul), died in July, whereupon Ryan was appointed.

3 Msgr. Lawrence F. Ryan, "Historical Sketch of the Cathedral of St. Paul, 1904-1937" (ACSP).

4 Msgr. Lawrence F. Ryan, "The Cathedral of St. Paul" (ACSP).

5 *Ibid.* Shortly after the dedication of the building on April 11, 1915, Ireland told the Diocesan Board of Consultors that "the interior completion of the Cathedral is assured. The income from the cathedral block for all the years that will be necessary will guarantee that." Ireland was referring to the site of the razed third Cathedral, which had been leased for ninety-nine years to an investment company. Unfortunately, his prediction was wide of the mark. Economic complications left the site vacant for many years, and by the time the Hamm Building was completed, the income was earmarked for other purposes (*Catholic Bulletin,* 17 October 1958).

6 *Catholic Bulletin,* 19 February 1916.

7 *Catholic Bulletin,* 14 February 1914. The projected inscription read, "This Chapel, dedicated to 'Our Lady,' is the affectionate offering of her daughters, the Catholic women of the Diocese of St. Paul."

8 *Catholic Bulletin,* 24 December 1927.

9 Mrs. Slade's rejection of the Baroque motif ultimately redounded to the credit of the Archbishop and the designer. As Henry Hope Reed, the noted architectural historian, told Msgr. Ryan,

> I am not certain of this, but I believe the original inspiration for all whorled columns comes from one of the Raphael tapestries now in the Vatican. Bernini used them for the baldachin in St. Peter's. There are several Gothic churches that have a modest version of whorling, notably St. Severin in Paris. Bishop [*sic*] Dowling and Whitney Warren created a new kind of baldachin by using the straight column (letter of 28 June 1955, in ACSP).

However, a more likely inspiration for Warren's original design was the baldachin in the Val-de-Grace, Paris. Designed by François Mansart and Jacques Lemercier, and built in 1645-1647, it would have been well-known to Warren, who, it will be remembered, had studied at the Ecole des Beaux-Arts.

10 *Catholic Bulletin,* 24 December 1927. It has also been claimed that the faces were modelled after those of Mrs. Slade's two daughters. What makes this version plausible is Slade's reaction after having been shown photographs of the angels for the first time. As her husband told Msgr. Ryan, "They impressed her so that one day when she was discussing her death and her last resting place, she told me that Mr. Warren could use the same designs for her monument. This he is now attempting to do..." (Slade to Ryan, 29 February 1924, in ACSP).

11 Christopher Tunnard and Henry Hope Reed, *American Skyline: The Growth and Forms of Our Cities and Towns* (Boston: Houghton Mifflin, 1955), 211.

12 Ryan, "Historical Sketch of the Cathedral of St. Paul, 1904-1937."

13 Franklin T. Ferguson, "The Cathedral of St. Paul," *Minnesota History* 39 (Winter 1964): 160.

14 The inscriptions are: "May your priests be clothed with justice; let your faithful ones shout merrily for joy" (Psalm 132:9); "Open to me the gates of justice; I will enter them and give thanks to the Lord" (Psalm 118:19); "Let us enter into his dwelling, let us worship at his footstool" (Psalm 132:7); "They shall come back rejoicing, carrying their sheaves" (Psalm 126:6); and, over the door leading into the apse, "Lift up, O ancient gates" (Psalm 24:9).

15 Ryan, "Historical Sketch of the Cathedral of St. Paul, 1904-1937."

16 *Ibid.*

17 *Catholic Bulletin,* 24 December 1927.

18 Archbishop John Ireland, *The New Cathedral of St. Paul; Letter of the Most Reverend Archbishop* (St. Paul: Privately Printed, 1905), n.p.

19 Though no official reason was ever given for the change, all the available material points to the following considerations: (1) St. Remy was virtually unkown, and thus lacked a following among the faithful; among the French of Minnesota, John the Baptist was a far more viable focus of devotion; (2) the number of English and Scandinavian Catholics in the state was negligible, while the growing Italian population could not be denied representation in the Cathedral; and (3) at the time of the work on the Shrines, St. Therese was at the peak of her popularity, having been canonized by Pius XI in May 1925. Interestingly, Msgr. Ryan always regretted the displacement of St. Ansgar (*St. Paul Pioneer Press,* 24 April 1966).

20 The chapel's two inscriptions refer rather pointedly to the intensity and beauty of her soul. The first reproduces her family's coat of arms, "I love ardently, I burn with passion for the Lord God of Hosts." The second is taken from the Song of Songs 7:6, "Your head rises like Carmel."

21 *St. Paul Pioneer Press,* 3 October 1920.

22 Archbishop John Ireland, *The Church and Modern Society; Lectures and Addresses* (St. Paul: The Pioneer Press, 1904-5), II, 58, 41.

23 Ireland, *The New Cathedral of St. Paul; Letter of the Most Reverend Archbishop,* n.p.

24 *Catholic Bulletin,* 7 and 21 March, and 2 May 1914.

25 Msgr. Lawrence F. Ryan, "Memorandum on Mankato Stone" (ACSP).

26 *Ibid.*

27 Ireland, *The New Cathedral of St. Paul; Letter of the Most Reverend Archbishop,* n.p. See also the *Catholic Bulletin,* 4 April 1914.

28 Entry of 8 December 1915, in "Minutes of the Meetings of the Executive Building Committee of the New Cathedral" (ACSP). The Committee made its judgement based on a few sample pages submitted by Mr. Salinger, the scribe. See also Ireland to Ryan, 12 December 1916 (ACSP). The volume was bound in tooled leather by Sister Philomene, C.S.J., around 1939.

29 See *infra,* Appendix One, 127.

30 James H. Moynihan, *The Life of Archbishop John Ireland* (New York: Harper & Brothers, 1953), 294. On the tenth anniversary of the visit, a bronze tablet, depicting Pacelli's preaching to the congregation, was placed in the wall near the pulpit.

Chapter Seven

1 On the life and work of Millet, who had served as chief of mural and decorative painting for the Louisiana Purchase Exposition in St. Louis, see Sharon S. Darling, *Chicago Ceramics & Glass* (Chicago: Chicago Historical Society, 1979), 17, 104-8.

2 Henry A. La Farge (son of Bancel) to Frederick F. Campbell, 25 August 1978 (ACSP).

3 Connick also designed windows for the Unity Church, the House of Hope, Nazareth Hall, and the Church of St. John the Evangelist, in St. Paul; the Hennepin Avenue Methodist Church, St. Mark's Episcopal Church, the Westminster Presbyterian Church, and the Plymouth Congregational Church, in Minneapolis; and the Buckham Memorial Library, in Faribault (Charles J. Connick, *Adventures in Light and Color; An Introduction to the Stained Glass Craft* [New York: Random House, 1937], 374).

4 Charles J. Connick, "The New East Rose Window" (ACSP).

5 Connick, *Adventures in Light and Color; An Introduction to the Stained Glass Craft,* 152.

6 *Ibid.,* 144.

7 Charles J. Connick, "The New East Rose Window in Saint Paul's Cathedral" (ACSP).

8 Connick to Ryan, 2 December 1940 (ACSP).

9 Chester A. Weston to Msgr. George E. Ryan, 20 November 1953 (ACSP). Masqueray's original designs called for clear glass in the

windows at the base of the dome. Exactly when and why his intention was abandoned, remains unclear.

10 *The Palm Beach Post,* 21 March 1987.

11 Louis W. Hill Papers, James J. Hill Reference Library, St. Paul, Minnesota.

12 On Ribot, see Robert Rosenblum and H.W. Janson, *19th Century Art* (New York: Abrams, 1984), 289; and *The Second Empire, 1852-1870: Art in France under Napoleon III* (Philadephia: Philadelphia Museum of Art, 1978), 350-1.

13 On Brewer, see Rena Neumann Coen, *Painting and Sculpture in Minnesota, 1820-1914* (Minneapolis: University of Minnesota Press, 1976), 78-9.

14 On Lehmann, see *The Second Empire, 1852-1870: Art in France under Napoleon III,* 324-5.

15 *St. Paul Sunday Pioneer Press,* 24 April 1966.

16 Entry 11 January 1907, in "Minutes of the Meetings of the Executive Building Committee of the New Cathedral" (ACSP).

17 Entries of 11 April and 3 October 1913, in *ibid.* The Berkey property was obtained by Archbishop Ireland for $35,000, a much lower price than that originally demanded by its owner.

18 Entry of 4 February 1914, in *ibid.;* Max Toltz to Charles H.F. Smith, 7 December 1915 (ACSP).

19 *Catholic Bulletin,* 15 April 1912.

20 James L. Esser, "The Cathedral of Saint Paul, St. Paul, Minnesota: An Architectural, Historical, and Descriptive Narrative" (Unpublished research paper, University of Minnesota, 1966), 46.

21 "Reminiscences of Thomas Kennedy (Undated)" (ACSP).

Chapter Eight

1 *Catholic Bulletin,* 17 October 1958.

2 See, for example, the *St. Paul Sunday Pioneer Press,* 24 April 1966.

3 "Reminiscences of Thomas Kennedy (Undated)" (ACSP).

4 *Catholic Bulletin,* 17 October 1958.

5 For the details of the ceremony, see *Consecration of the Cathedral of Saint Paul, St. Paul, Minnesota, October 14, 1958, by the Most Reverend William O. Brady, S.T.D., Archbishop of St. Paul* (ACSP).

6 *Catholic Bulletin,* 13 December 1974.

7 Msgr. Lawrence F. Ryan, "Historical Sketch of the Cathedral of St. Paul, 1904-1937" (ACSP).

8 *Catholic Bulletin,* 20 August 1976 and 25 March 1977.

9 *Catholic Bulletin,* 20 August 1976.

10 See, for example, the comments by Msgr. Lawrence F. Ryan, cited in the *Catholic Bulletin,* 2 February 1968.

Conclusion

1 *St. Paul Sunday Pioneer Press,* 24 April 1966.

2 James L. Esser, "The Cathedral of Saint Paul, St. Paul, Minnesota: An Architectural, Historical, and Descriptive Narrative" (Unpublished research paper, University of Minnesota, 1966), 51-2.

3 Letter to Henry Wilberforce, 24 September 1846, in *The Letters and Diaries of John Henry Newman,* Vol. XI: *Littlemore to Rome, October 1845 to December 1846,* ed. Charles Stephen Dessain (London: Thomas Nelson & Sons, 1961), 253. Newman made the observation after a visit to the fourteenth-century Cathedral of Milan.

4 Jim Fabricius to Msgr. Ambrose V. Hayden, 7 October 1983 (ACSP).

5 *Catholic Bulletin,* 2 February 1968.

6 "The Laying of the Corner Stone of The New Cathedral," *Acta et Dicta* 1 (July 1907): 100; Msgr. Lawrence F. Ryan, Untitled memoir on the Cathedral of Saint Paul (ACSP).

7 *St. Paul Pioneer Press,* 24 April 1966.

8 Cited in Shane Leslie, *Cardinal Gasquet; A Memoir* (London: Burns Oates, 1953), 44.

APPENDIX ONE

REMEMBERED IN THIS CATHEDRAL OF ST. PAUL
ARE THE ARCHBISHOPS, BISHOPS AND PASTORS
WHO HAVE SERVED THIS CHURCH
FROM ITS FOUNDING AS A CHAPEL, NOV. 1ST 1841.

BISHOPS

+ JOSEPH CRETIN	1851-1857
+ THOMAS L. GRACE	1859-1884
+ JOHN IRELAND	1884-1888

ARCHBISHOPS

+ JOHN IRELAND	1888-1918
+ AUSTIN DOWLING	1919-1930
+ JOHN G. MURRAY	1931-1956
+ WILLIAM O. BRADY	1956-1961
+ LEO BINZ	1961-1975
+ LEO C. BYRNE, COADJUTOR	1967-1974
+ JOHN R. ROACH	1975-

PASTORS

LUCIEN GALTIER	1841-1844
AUGUSTINE RAVOUX	1844-1851
+ JOSEPH CRETIN	1851-1856
DENNIS LEDON	1856-1857
AUGUSTINE RAVOUX	1857-1859
+ THOMAS L. GRACE	1859-1861
LOUIS E. CAILLET	1861-1867
JOHN IRELAND	1867-1875
JOHN SHANLEY	1875-1889
PATRICK R. HEFFRON	1890-1896
+ JOHN J. LAWLER	1896-1916
THOMAS J. GIBBONS	1916-
LAWRENCE F. RYAN	1916-1940
JOHN J. CULLINAN	1940-1942
FRANCIS J. SCHENK	1942-1945
GEORGE E. RYAN	1945-1960
+ GERALD F. O'KEEFE	1961-1967
AMBROSE V. HAYDEN	1967-

The West Wall of the Founders' Chapel

APPENDIX TWO

The Work of Emmanuel L. Masqueray

The following list includes only some of Masqueray's commissions, arranged in approximate chronological order. The absence of dates for certain entries indicates that the precise years of design and construction are at this point unkown. A complete and detailed listing of Masqueray's architectural output will be possible only if and when his personal papers, which he bequeathed to the Catholic Historical Society of St. Paul, are returned to the Society's Archives, from which they have inexplicably disappeared.

Basilica of St. Mary, Minneapolis (1906-1914)

Cathedral of St. Paul, St. Paul (1906-1915)

Church of St. Louis, St. Paul (1907-1913)

Cathedral of the Immaculate Conception, Wichita (1908- 1912)

Church of St. Teresa, Hutchinson, Kansas (1909)

Ireland Hall, College of St. Thomas, St. Paul (1910-1912)

Church of St. Peter, St. Peter, Minnesota (1911)

Grace Residence Hall, St. Paul Seminary, St. Paul

St. Joseph Novitiate, College of St. Catherine, St. Paul (1911-1912)

Church of St. Martin, Rogers, Minnesota (1912)

St. Paul's Episcopal Church-on-the-Hill, St. Paul (1912)

Church of St. Edward the Confessor, Minneota, Minnesota (1912-1914)

Church of St. Mary, Waverly, Iowa

Church of St. Martin, Huron, South Dakota (1913-1914)

Church of St. Mary, Manchester, Iowa

Bethlehem Lutheran Church, St. Paul (1914)

Church of St. Wilfrid, Woonsocket, South Dakota (1914- 1915)

Cathedral of St. Mary, Winnipeg, Manitoba

Church of the Immaculate Conception, Van Horne, Iowa (1915)

Church of St. Patrick, Cedar Falls, Iowa

Church of the Holy Redeemer, St. Paul (1915-1916)

Church of St. Benedict, Decorah, Iowa

Church of St. Joseph, Cresco, Iowa

Church of St. Mary, Waucoma, Iowa

Church of the Holy Redeemer, Marshall, Minnesota (1916)

Church of St. Anne, Somerset, Wisconsin (1916-1917)

Cathedral of St. Joseph, Sioux Falls, South Dakota (1916- 1919)

Chapel of the College of St. Thomas, St. Paul (1917-1918)

Church of the Incarnation, Minneapolis (1916-1920)

Church of St. Francis Xavier, Benson, Minnesota (1917)

APPENDIX THREE

Dimensions of the Cathedral of Saint Paul

(Source: *Catholic Bulletin, Cathedral Supplement,* 10 April 1915)

Exterior

Length — 307 feet (including front steps, 37 feet)
Width of transepts — 216 feet
Height of walls — 80 feet
Height of gables in transepts, above foundation
　　walls — 103 feet
Height to cornice in dome — 148 feet
Height to base of cross — 292 feet
Height above floor to top of cross — 306½ feet
Diameter of dome — 120 feet
Diameter of rose windows — 26 feet

Facade

Width — 143 feet
Height above foundation walls to base of cross —
　　114 feet
Height to top of cross — 124 feet
Height of main arch — 76 feet
Height of towers — 164 feet
Width of central door — 12 feet
Width of side doors — 6 feet
Sculptures — Science and Religion, over front
　　entrance — 27 feet long by 8 feet high
　　Christ and the Apostles, above main arch — 60
　　feet wide
　　Statues of St. Peter and St. Paul — 12 feet high

Interior

Width of nave — 60 feet
Width of ambulatory — 12 feet
Height of nave ceiling above floor — 83 feet
Height of dome ceiling — 186 feet
Diameter of dome — 96 feet
Sanctuary — 60 feet by 62 feet
Narthex — 16 feet deep by 62 feet wide
Chapels — Blessed Virgin Mary — 36 feet deep by
　　22 feet wide
　　St. Joseph — 36 feet deep by 22 feet wide
　　St. Peter — 26 feet deep by 22 feet wide
　　Sacred Heart — 26 feet deep by 22 feet wide
Shrines of the Nations — each 13 feet deep by 15
　　feet wide
Founders' Chapel — 16 feet deep by 16 feet wide
Baptistry — 16 feet deep by 16 feet wide
Seating capacity — Nave and transepts — 2,400
　　Nave, transepts, chapels, and ambulatory — 3,500

APPENDIX FOUR

A Walking Tour of the Cathedral of Saint Paul

Numbers in parentheses refer to pages featuring a history, description, and/or illustration of the particular item.

1   Baptistry (75, 76, 93), with south tower and bells above (111, 113-14)
2   lunette of the Annuciation (87)
3   Chapel of the Blessed Virgin Mary (52, 53, 81-2, 108)
4   St. Mark (97, 100)
5   Brewer, *Crucifixion* (97, 98)
6   lunette of the hierarchy (92-3)
7   lower transept windows, St. Anthony Mary Claret/St. Pius X (94-95)
8   south rose window (87-9)
9   confessional windows: St. John Vianney/the Christ of Revelation/St. Mary Magdalene (90-2)
10 lunette of the Papacy (92-3)
11 Chapel of St. Peter (44-6, 81)
12 St. Matthew (97, 100)
13 ambulatory (70-1)
14 *Te Deum* and *Magnificat* grilles (58, 60, 62-3)
15 Shrine of St. Anthony (63, 66, 82, 83)
16 Shrine of St. John the Baptist (63, 67, 83)
17 Shrine of St. Patrick (63, 64, 83-4)
18 sacristy entrance, with console grille above (70, 71)
19 sacristy vestibule
20 sacristy (56-7, 58, 59, 95-6)
21 Shrine of St. Boniface (63, 65, 84)
22 Shrine of Sts. Cyril and Methodius (63, 68, 70, 83, 84)
23 Shrine of St. Therese (69, 70, 84)
24 St. John (97, 100)

25 plaques honoring Pacelli and Murray (108)
26 apse (52, 54-6)
27 windows of the Sacraments (84-5)
28 pulpit (58-61)
29 Ribot, *The Entombment* (96-7)
30 choir stalls (58, 60)
31 sanctuary organ (101)
32 main altar and baldachin (52, 54-6)
33 *cathedra* (1)
34 bronze seal of the Archdiocese of St. Paul and Minneapolis (58, 60)
35 altar railing (58)
36 dome, with windows of Angels (94-5, 96), chandelier (101), and mosaics of the virtues (107-8)
37 plaque in memory of John F. Kennedy (109)
38 Chapel of the Sacred Heart (72, 84)
39 lunette of the clergy (92-3)
40 north rose window (89-90, 91)
41 confessional windows: St. John Nepomucene/Christ the Good Shepherd/St. Dismas (92, 93)
42 lunette of the laity (92-3)
43 lower transept windows: St. Maria Goretti/St. John Bosco (94)
44 St. Luke (97, 101)
45 Lehmann, *The Descent from the Cross* (97, 99)
46 lunette of the Presentation (90, 91)
47 Chapel of St. Joseph (46, 81, 108)
48 Founders' Chapel (75, 77, 93, 94), with north tower above
49 narthex (75, 93-4), with organ gallery above (101)
50 east rose window (85-7)

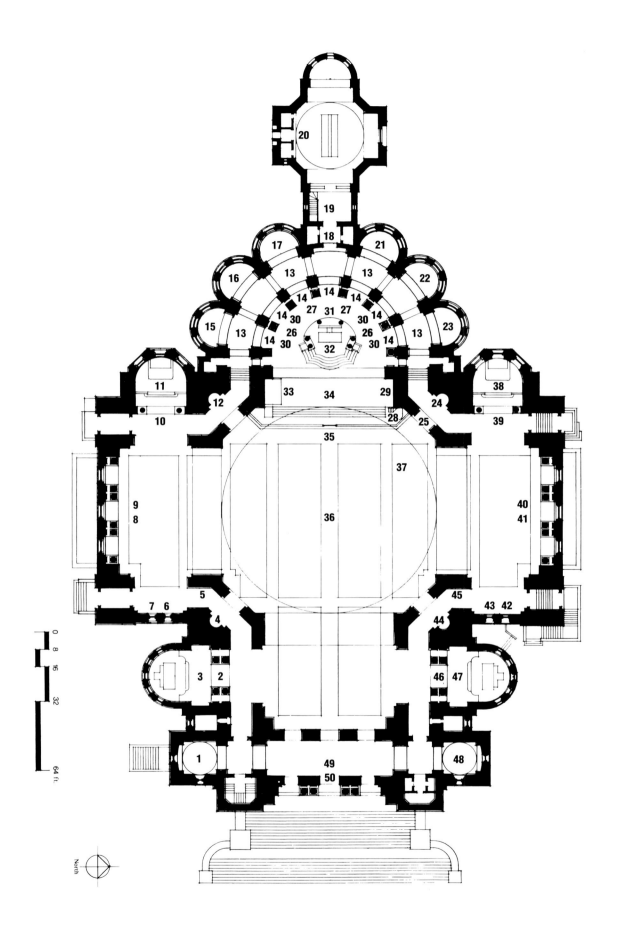

North

APPENDIX FIVE

Architects, Designers, and Contractors of the Cathedral of Saint Paul

The following list, though not complete, represents the major portion of the total number of groups and individuals who have contributed their skills to the Cathedral fabric and its embellishment over the past seventy-five years.

Architects and Designers

Emmanuel Louis Masqueray, Chief Architect

Charles D. Maginnis and Timothy Walsh (interior decor, Chapel of the Sacred Heart)

Whitney Warren (baldachin)

McBride and Gorham (main altar)

Leon Hermant (pedimental sculpture of the facade, interior statuary: St. Peter, St. Joseph, Blessed Virgin with Child)

Pennell, Gibbs, and Quiring (decoration of the upper sanctuary)

Ernest Pellegrini (angel atop the sacristy dome)

Albert H. Atkins (pulpit, sanctuary grilles, interior statuary: St. Boniface, St. Anthony, St. John the Baptist, St. Therese)

Sidney W. Woollett (interior statuary: St. Patrick, Sacred Heart)

Alban Polasek (interior statuary: Saints Cyril and Methodius)

John Garratti (symbols above the interior doors of the transepts)

Carl Carlquist (confessionals)

Louis J. Millet (windows of the Chapels of St. Peter, St. Joseph, and the Blessed Virgin)

Bancel La Farge (windows of the Shrines of the Nations and the Chapel of the Sacred Heart)

Charles J. Connick (upper sanctuary windows, east rose window, lunette of the Chapel of the Blessed Virgin Mary, north and south rose windows)

Connick Associates (lunette of the Chapel of St. Joseph, confessional windows)

Chester A. Weston (transept, lunettes, baptistry and Founders' Chapel windows, windows in the lower eastern walls of the transepts, windows in the dome)

Conrad Pickel (sacristy windows)

St. Paul Statuary Company/Giuliani Statuary Company (interior decoration and carving)

John Angel (statues of the Four Evangelists)

Brioschi & Son (ornamental stone elements in the transepts and under the choir gallery)

Ernest Skinner Company (sanctuary organ)

Aeolian-Skinner Company (choir gallery organ)

Joseph A. Capecchi (main ceiling decoration, Stations of the Cross, consecration crosses, tympana above the interior doors of the transepts)

Michelangelo Bedini (pendentive mosaics)

Frank Kacmarcik (inscription at base of dome)

Contractors

Lauer Brothers Construction Company (excavation and foundation to water table)

P.M. Hennessy Construction Company (superstructure)

St. Paul Cement Works

St. Paul Foundry (steel)

W.J. Hoy Company (steelwork for towers, dome, and steps)

Thomas Finn Roofing Company (copper roofing)

Butler Brothers (caulking)

Beil & Hermant (ceiling of roof and dome)

Minuti Brothers (plasterwork)

E.M. Lohmann Company (marble for the Chapel of St. Joseph)

William Poppenberger & Son (interior plasterwork)

Toltz Engineering Company (heating and ventilation)

Dubuque Altar Manufacturing Company (pews)

Fielding and Shelby (grading)

Portland Stone Company (sidewalks)

Foley Brothers (sacristy and rectory)

Drake Marble and Tile Company (marble for the Chapel of the Sacred Heart)

C.H. Young Company/T.R. Coughlan Company (Mankato stone for the interior)

Isco Corporation (insulation of the roof)

Bettenburg, Townsend, Stolte, and Comb (north side of the crypt)

Rambusch and Company (current interior lighting system)

McGough Construction Company (preparation of south tower for bells)

Paccard Foundry (five bells for the south tower)

Voigt and Fourre (installation of bells)

BIBLIOGRAPHY

Unpublished Sources

Archives of the Catholic Historical Society of St. Paul
Archives of the Cathedral of Saint Paul
Louis W. Hill Papers, James J. Hill Reference Library, St. Paul

Published Sources

Books

Ahern, Patrick, ed. *Catholic Heritage in Minnesota, North Dakota, and South Dakota.* St. Paul: The Province of St. Paul, 1964.

Coen, Rena Neumann. *Painting and Sculpture in Minnesota, 1820-1914.* Minneapolis: University of Minnesota Press, 1976.

Connick, Charles J. *Adventures in Light and Color; An Introduction to the Stained Glass Craft.* New York: Random House, 1937.

Darling, Sharon S. *Chicago Ceramics & Glass.* Chicago: Chicago Historical Society, 1979.

Gray, Robert. *Cardinal Manning; A Biography.* London: Weidenfeld and Nicolson, 1985.

Ireland, Archbishop John. *The Church and Modern Society; Lectures and Addresses.* 2 vols. St. Paul: The Pioneer Press, 1904-5.

Leslie, Shane. *Cardinal Gasquet; A Memoir.* London: Burns Oates, 1953.

Moynihan, James H. *The Life of Archbishop John Ireland.* New York: Harper & Brothers, 1953.

Newman, John Henry. *The Letters and Diaries of John Henry Newman.* Vol. XI: *Littlemore to Rome, October 1845 to December 1846.* Edited by Charles Stephen Dessain. London: Thomas Nelson & Sons, 1961.

O'Connell, Marvin R. *John Ireland and the American Catholic Church.* St. Paul: Minnesota Historical Society Press, 1988.

Reardon, James M. *The Catholic Church in the Diocese of St. Paul from Earliest Origins to Centennial Achievement.* St. Paul: North Central Publishing Company, 1952.

Rosenblum, Robert, and Janson, H.W. *19th-Century Art.* New York: Abrams, 1984.

The Second Empire, 1852-1870: Art in France under Napoleon III. Philadephia: Philadephia Museum of Art, 1978.

Tunnard, Christopher, and Reed, Henry Hope. *American Skyline: The Growth and Forms of Our Cities and Towns.* Boston: Houghton Mifflin, 1955.

Articles

Ferguson, Franklin T. "The Cathedral of St. Paul." *Minnesota History* 39 (Winter 1964): 153-62.

Ireland, Archbishop John. "Sermon Presented at the Final Service of the Old Cathedral of St. Paul." *Acta et Dicta* 4 (July 1915): 79-93.

Lathrop, Alan K. "A French Architect in Minnesota: Emmanuel L. Masqueray, 1861-1917." *Minnesota History* 46 (Summer 1980): 42-56.

"The Laying of the Corner Stone of The New Cathedral." *Acta et Dicta* 1 (July 1907): 99-151

McNulty, A. "The Chapel of St. Paul, The Cradle of the Catholic Church in Minnesota." *Acta et Dicta* 1 (July 1907): 60-72.

Masqueray, E.L. "Religious Architecture and the Cathedral of St. Paul and Pro-Cathedral of the Immaculate Conception." *Western Architect* 12 (October 1908): 43-4.

"Meeting of the Board of Consultors (Address of the Archbishop)." *The New Cathedral Bulletin* 1 (August 1904): 10-12.

"The New Cathedral." *Acta et Dicta* 3 (July 1914): 322-38.

"The New Cathedral." *The New Cathedral Bulletin* 1 (August 1904): 1-2.

Oster, Anatole. "Personal Reminiscences of Bishop Cretin." *Acta et Dicta* 1 (July 1907): 73-88.

Pamphlets and Reports

Esser, James L. "The Cathedral of Saint Paul, St. Paul, Minnesota: An Architectural, Historical and Descriptive Narrative." Unpublished research paper, University of Minnesota, 1966.

Ireland, Archbishop John. *The New Cathedral of St. Paul; Letter of the Most Reverend Archbishop.* St. Paul: Privately Printed, 1905.

Reardon, James M. ed. *Archbishop Ireland: Prelate-Patriot-Publicist, 1838-1918; A Memoir.* St. Paul: The Catholic Bulletin, n.d.

Newspapers

Catholic Bulletin. 1911-77.
Midway News. 1889-90.
Northwestern Chronicle. 1887-1906.
The Palm Beach Post. 1987.
St. Paul Dispatch. 1910.
St. Paul Pioneer Press. 1905-66.

INDEX

Albert, J. Howard, 37
ambulatory, 70. fig. 6.25
Anderson, Oscar, 40
Angel, John, 97
Atkins, Albert H., 58, 62, 63, 70

baldachin, 46, 52, 54, 56, 125 (6⁹⁻¹⁰), figs. 6.4, 6.5, 6.6
baptistry, 75, 93, fig. 6.31
Bedini, Michelangelo, 107
Beil & Hermant, 43
bells, 111, 113-14, figs. 8.10, 8.12
Berkey property, 31, 124 (4²)
Bertozzi, Egisto, 97
Bettenburg, Townsend, Stolte, and Comb, 108
Blessed Virgin and Child (Hermant), 52, fig. 6.3
Board of Consultors, 19-20, 123 (3¹²)
Bremer, Otto, 37
Brewer, Nicholas Richard, 97
Brioschi and Son, 108

Capecchi, Joseph A., 106, 108
cathedra, 1
Cathedrals of Saint Paul
    first (1851), 11-12, fig. 2.3
    second (1851-8), 12-13, fig. 2.5
    third (1858-1914), 13-14, 43-4, figs. 2.6, 5.1
    fourth (opened 1915). *See also* Ireland, John, first
        Archbishop of St. Paul; Masqueray, Emmanuel Louis
    selection and adjustment of site, 19, 31, fig. 4.1
    fund-raising, 25-7, 36, 124 (3³⁶)
    cost, 31-2, 117
    work on foundation, 33-4, figs. 4.3, 4.4
    crypt, 33-4, 46, 48, 56, 108, 111
    construction of exterior, 34, 36-7, 37-9, figs. 4.7, 4.8
    early criticism of, 31, 36, 44
    placement of roof and dome, 37-8, figs. 4.9, 4.10
    facade, 39-40, figs. 3.4, 3.7, 4.11, 4.12, 4.13
    first Mass, 43, 44, 125 (5⁸)
    completion of interior, 44-6, 52-6, 57-8, 63, 70-2, 74-5,
        105-8, 125 (6⁵), fig. 6.29
    consecration (1958), 108-9, fig. 8.6
    listed in National Register of Historical Buildings, 111
    vandalism, 111
    restoration of 1977, 111, fig. 8.9
    future projects, 117
    its symbolism, 117-19
    dimensions, 129
    walking tour, 130-1
Chapels
    of St. Peter, 44-6, 81, figs. 5.2, 5.3, 7.1
    of St. Joseph, 46, 81, 90, 108, fig. 5.4
    of the Blessed Virgin Mary, 52, 53, 81-2, 87, 108, 125 (6⁷),
        figs. 6.3, 7.2
    of the Sacred Heart, 72, 84, fig. 6.28
choir stalls, 58, fig. 6.14

Christ and the Apostles Flanked by Saints Peter and Paul
    (Hermant), 39-40, fig. 4.12
Clark & McCormack, 34, 36
confessionals, 77
confessional windows, 90, 92, figs. 7.22, 7.23
Connick, Charles J., 84-90, 126 (7³)
consecration of the fourth Cathedral (1958), 108-9, fig. 8.6
Cretin, Joseph, first Bishop of St. Paul, 12-13, 52, fig. 2.4
Crucifixion (Brewer), 97, fig. 7.30
Cullinan, Monsignor John J., 105
Descent from the Cross, The (Lehmann), 97, fig. 7.31
dome, 37-8, 94-5, 105-7, 118, 126 (7⁹), figs. 3.6, 3.7, 4.9, 4.10,
    7.26, 8.2
Dowling, Austin, second Archbishop of St. Paul, 51, 52, 54,
    56, 72, 83, fig. 6.1
Drake Marble and Tile Company, 72

East Rose Window *(The Resurrection),* 85-7, figs. 7.9, 7.10,
    7.11
Entombment, The (Ribot), 96-7, fig. 7.29
Executive Building Committee, 20-1, 25-6, 31, 33-4, 37, 123
    (3¹⁶), fig. 3.2

Faith and Science (Anderson), 39, 40, fig. 4.13
Foley Brothers, 25, 56
Fortitude (Bedini), 107
Founders' Chapel, 75, 77, 93, 127, fig. 7.24. *See also*
    memorial volume (Founders' Chapel)
Fuzet, François Cardinal, Archbishop of Rouen, 23

Galeazzi, Count Enrico, 78
Galtier, Father Lucien, 11-12, fig. 2.1
Garratti, John, 39
Gibbons, Father Thomas J., 125 (6²), fig. 3.2
Grace, Thomas Langdon, O.P., second Bishop of St. Paul, 14,
    fig. 2.7

Hayden, Monsignor Ambrose V., 111
heating system, 100-1
Hennessy Construction Company, P.M., 37
Hermant, Leon, 39-40, 45, 46, 52
Hill, Louis W., 20, 25
Hoy Company, W.J., 37

Ireland, John, first Archbishop of St. Paul
    his decision to build the Cathedral, 5, 123 (3⁹)
    personality, religious outlook, and accomplishments, 5-7
    his first meeting with Masqueray, 8
    his selection of the Cathedral site, 19
    fund-raising and publicity efforts for the Cathedral, 25-7,
        36, 37-8
    celebrates first Mass in Cathedral, 44, 125 (5⁸)
    final months, death, and funeral, 46, 48, fig. 5.6
    his respect for the construction team, 117, figs. 1.1, 3.2
Isco Corporation, 105

Joan of Arc, 70
Justice (Bedini), 107, fig. 8.3

Kennedy, John F., 109, fig. 8.7
Kittson Mansion, 19, fig. 3.1

La Farge, Bancel, 82-4
Larpenteur, A.L., 20
Lauer Brothers Construction Company, 33
Lawler, Father (later Bishop) John J., 36, 125 (6²), figs. 3.2, 4.6
laying of the cornerstone (1907), 29-30, 34-6, fig. 4.5
Lehmann, Karl-Ernest-Rodolphe-Heinrich-Salem, 97
Lohmann Company, E.M., 46
lighting system
    interior, 101, fig. 7.36
    exterior, 111, fig. 8.8
Loras, Mathias, Bishop of Dubuque, 11, 12
lunettes
    of the Annunciation, 87
    of the Presentation, 90, fig. 7.21
    in the transepts, 92-3
McGolrick, James, Bishop of Duluth, 35, 44
McNair, H.C., 19, fig. 3.2
Maginnis and Walsh, 21, 56
main altar, 54, 56, figs. 6.4, 6.5
Masqueray, Emmanuel Louis
    training and pre-1904 career, 7-8
    his first meeting with Ireland, 8
    selection as Cathedral architect, 21-3
    projected plans for the Cathedral, 23-5, figs. 3.3, 3.4, 3.5, 3.6
    his work with Ireland and the Executive Committee, 31, 33, 36
    death and funeral, 46
    his major ecclesiastical commissions, 128, figs. 1.2, 5.5
Meagher, John B., 20
memorial volume (Founders' Chapel), 75, 77, 126 (6²⁸), figs. 6.32, 6.33
Millet, Louis J., 81-2
mosaics of the Virtues, 107-8, figs. 8.3, 8.4
Murray, John Gregory, third Archbishop of St. Paul, 72, figs. 6.27, 6.34

narthex, 75, 93-4, fig. 6.30
North Rose Window (The American Jesuit Martyrs), 89-90. figs. 7.16, 7.17, 7.18, 7.19, 7.20

O'Connell, Rose Ann, 58
O'Gorman, Thomas, Bishop of Sioux Falls, 43, 44
O'Keefe, Gerald F., Bishop of Davenport, 109, fig. 8.7
organs, 70, 101, fig. 6.26

Pacelli, Eugenio Cardinal, 77-8, fig. 6.34
Paschal candlestick, 115-16
Pellegrini, Ernest, 56
Pennell, Gibbs, and Quiring, 58
Piccirilli, 97
Pickel, Conrad, 95-6
Polasek, Alban, 63
Prudence (Bedini), 107
pulpit, 58, fig. 6.15

Ravoux, Father Augustine, 12-14, fig. 2.2
rectory, 56
Ribot, Théodule-Augustin, 96-7
Riley, William C., 117

Roach, John R., seventh Archbishop of St. Paul and Minneapolis, 111, fig. 8.11
Ryan, Monsignor George E., 105, 113, 117-18, 124 (3³⁶), figs. 8.1, 8.6
Ryan, Monsignor Lawrence F., 51-2, fig. 6.2
Sacred Heart, The (Woollett), 72, fig. 6.28
sacristy, 56-7, 95-6, 125 (6¹⁴), figs. 6.7, 6.8, 6.9, 6.10, 6.11, 7.27, 7.28
St. Anthony (Atkins), 63, fig. 6.21
St. Boniface (Atkins), 63, fig. 6.20
St. John (Angel/Bertozzi), 97, fig. 7.34
St. John the Baptist (Atkins), 63, fig. 6.22
St. Joseph (Hermant), 46, fig. 5.4
St. Luke (Angel/Piccirilli), 97, fig. 7.35
St. Mark (Angel/Piccirilli), 97, fig. 7.32
St. Matthew (Angel/Bertozzi), 97, fig. 7.33
St. Patrick (Woollett), 63, fig. 6.19
St. Paul Statuary Company, 111
St. Peter (Hermant), 41-2, 45, fig. 5.2
St. Therese (Atkins), 70, fig. 6.24
Sts. Cyril and Methodius (Polasek), 63, 70, fig. 6.23
sanctuary, 58, 84-5, figs. 6.13, 7.7, 7.8. See also Te Deum and Magnificat grilles (Atkins)
Satolli, Francesco Cardinal, 19
Schenk, Bishop Francis J., 105
Selby Avenue tunnel, 31, fig. 4.2
Seven Gifts of the Holy Spirit, The (Pennell, Gibbs, and Quiring), 58, fig. 6.12
Shrines
    of St. Anthony, 63, 83, figs. 6.21, 7.3
    of St. Boniface, 63, 84, fig. 6.20
    of Sts. Cyril and Methodius, 63, 70, 84, figs. 6.23, 7.6
    of St. John the Baptist, 63, 83, fig. 6.22
    of St. Patrick, 63, 83-4, figs. 6.19, 7.4, 7.5
    of St. Therese, 70, 84, 126 (6²⁰), fig. 6.24
Slade, Georgiana, 56
Slade, Mrs. George Theron (née Charlotte Hill), 52, 54
Slifer and Abrahamson, 56
Smiraldi, 54
Smith, Charles H.F., 19, 20, 25, fig. 3.2
sound system, 101
South Rose Window (The Beatitudes), 87-9, figs. 7.12, 7.13, 7.14, 7.15
Stations of the Cross (Capecchi), 108, fig. 8.5
Stickney, A.B., 19

Te Deum and Magnificat grilles (Atkins), 58, 60, 62-3, figs. 6.16, 6.17, 6.18
Temperance (Bedini), 107, fig. 8.4
Toltz Engineering Company, 101
transept lunettes, 92-3
transept windows, 94, fig. 7.25
Twin City Ornamental Iron and Bronze Company, 58

"Vannutelli lintel," 37, 124 (4³²)
vestibules, 75

Warren, Whitney, 52, 54, 56
Weston, Chester A., 92-5
Woollett, Sidney W., 63, 72

Young Company, C.H., 72

The Cathedral of Saint Paul: The Selby Avenue Side